# How to Repair
# and Maintain Your
# Apple Computer

# How to Repair and Maintain Your Apple Computer

## All II Series Models, Including the IIc

**Gene B. Williams**

CHILTON BOOK COMPANY

Radnor, Pennsylvania

When it comes down to it, the two people more responsible than any others for this book are my parents.

The book is also dedicated to my wife, Cindy, who only rarely interrupted with, ''Don't you think it's about time to take a break away from that computer?''

Copyright © 1985 by Gene B. Williams
All Rights Reserved
Published in Radnor, Pennsylvania 19089 by Chilton Book Company
Designed by Arlene Putterman
Manufactured in the United States of America

Library of Congress Cataloging in Publication Data
Williams, Gene B.
    How to repair and maintain your Apple computer
  (Chilton's business computing series)
  Includes index
  1. Microcomputers—Maintenance and repair.
2. Apple computer.   I. Title.   II. Series.
TK7887.W549  1985      001.64      84-45353
ISBN 0-8019-7623-5 (wire-o with disk)
ISBN 0-8019-7549-2 (pbk.)
ISBN 0-8019-7640-5

Chilton's Business Computing Series

    4 5 6 7 8 9 0    4 3 2 1 0 9 8 7

# Contents

*Williams: How to Repair & Maintain Your Apple Computer (Chilton)*

*Williams: How to Repair & Maintain Your Apple Computer (Chilton)*

*Williams: How to Repair & Maintain Your Apple Computer (Chilton)*

======================================

# Preface

A few years ago, I bought my first computer. I was facing a tight deadline. The computer had been checked out before I packed it into my car and brought it to the office. Back in the office, it was plugged in, booted up with the program. Nothing! The screen was blank.

I called the seller to explain the problem. He said that he couldn't be out until the following Wednesday. So much for my deadline. The only solution was to try a diagnosis by phone.

He told me to open the case. I was convinced that the second I did that, the machine would be ruined for all time. A look inside confirmed my fears. There seemed to be several hundred memory boards along with enough mysterious components to launch the next deep space probe. I had about as much desire to touch the insides of the machine as I have to jump out of a moving car.

Under the dealer's direction, each board was pulled, cleaned, and inserted back into the mother board. What should have been a 30-second job took 30 minutes. I was so sure that every movement would break something important that I did everything very slowly.

I tried to get the computer to operate again, thinking that a reset might cure the trouble. Absolutely nothing! The dealer repeated, "I really can't make it there before Wednesday. Oh, by the way, have you checked the contrast control? Maybe you bumped it."

*Williams: How to Repair & Maintain Your Apple Computer (Chilton)*

"Contrast control? What contrast control?"

"It's on the left, beneath the keyboard."

I reached under and felt a little wheel. "You mean that little wheel thingy?"

Suddenly the screen came to life with all the signs and symbols it was supposed to display. The problem was solved and I met the deadline.

As the months went by, I ran into other problems. With each, I went through the same feelings of helplessness. A computer is an extremely complicated piece of machinery, isn't it? Doesn't a person need years of training and experience, plus a room full of special tools and test equipment, to repair such a machine?

Most of my problems turned out to be minor. I usually handled repair with tools no more complex than a screwdriver. A few times, I had to get "technical" and use an ordinary voltmeter.

Then I became involved with other computers. The knowledge I'd gained from my first computer carried over. From conversations with other computer owners, I found that most not only knew very little about their machines but also were on the verge of being terrified of them.

As a result, this handbook and guide was developed. It will help you in taking care of the most common failures in a personal computer system. With rare exception, the typical person *can* do it. A computer is not all that grand and mysterious. It's just a machine—sophisticated perhaps, but a machine all the same. There are only so many reasons why a machine fails to work.

Most of the repair steps are identical for all Apple models. When there is a major difference, it is noted in the text, photos, and drawings.

If you're standing in a bookstore reading this, keep in mind that this book aims to save you *at least* ten times its cost. More important to some, it will save you a great deal of time, both in waiting for the technician and in driving to and from the shop. BUY IT! If you've already bought this book, congratulations! You won't regret it.

My thanks go to several people who were helpful in putting this book together for you. Collaborator, technician, and all-around good guy James Wennmacher provided the needed technical support. Without his input, it just wouldn't have been the same. Moral supporter and the driving force behind the project was Phil Good. Then there are Bill Belisle and Tom Kay, both of whom are responsible for getting me involved with computers in the first place.

*Williams: How to Repair & Maintain Your Apple Computer (Chilton)*

# Introduction

Before the Apple computer was introduced, the world of computing was more or less confined to big business. The average person couldn't hope to afford a computer. Special schooling was needed to operate one. Apple was one of the companies that changed all this.

The growing popularity of home computers is due largely to the fact that they are becoming easier and easier to operate. Not many years ago, the person who had a home computer was thought to be a genius (or a "nut"). There were very few commercial programs available, which meant that the owner of a home computer had to have a solid knowledge of programming.

Ask any ten people today. Several will own a computer. More yet will be in the category, "We're thinking about it." Nine out of ten are likely to have some kind of computer around—a pocket calculator if nothing else.

Almost anyone can operate a computer. You might enjoy your computer more if you learn some programming, but all you really need are preprogrammed diskettes. Push one in, press a few buttons, and you're ready to go.

Meanwhile, the cost for technical work such as repair and installation of add-ons has jumped. Charges of $60 per hour or more for labor alone are common. Some shops charge a $150 minimum just for looking at a malfunctioning machine. Should the computer owner need the technician to come to his or her home or place of business, all costs increase.

Average downtime for a repair is three days. Having the machine tied up for a week or more isn't unusual.

*Williams: How to Repair & Maintain Your Apple Computer (Chilton)*

To avoid these high costs and inconveniences, some owners purchase a repair contract. Typical yearly cost is betwen 5% and 10% of the purchase price. A fee of 20% isn't unheard of. Several sources list a cost of 1% per month as the minimum to be expected without such a contract.

To make things even more depressing, it has been said that 95% of all repairs and other technical work could be taken care of by the computer owner without special tools or technical background. About two-thirds of all repairs require nothing more complicated than your fingers. For the other one-third, it's rare that you'll need anything but simple, ordinary tools you probably have already. (See "Tools You'll Need" at the end of the introduction.) There is often no need for you to spend hundreds of dollars; to wait a week, or even a day, while the repair is being done; or to waste time going to and from the shop.

## ADVANTAGES OF THIS BOOK

The purpose of this book is to show you just how easy it is to diagnose and repair most malfunctions. It will also show you how easy it is to maintain a system properly in order to reduce repairs. You don't need a knowledge of electronics. It helps, but you can handle many repairs without it.

Chapter 1 acquaints you with the rules of the game. Its purpose is to show you what can cause trouble or damage, both to you and to the computer. Dangerous spots are revealed to prevent you from getting a shock. Cautions and precautions are given to keep you from making costly mistakes. If you read this chapter thoroughly and use the information in it, you are highly unlikely to run into trouble while working on your computer.

Chapter 2 shows you how to diagnose malfunctions and how to get your computer to diagnose itself with the help of a diagnostics diskette. (A computer is a powerful tool, if you let it be one. The IIe even has a built-in self-test that runs a quick computer check). This chapter provides tips on how to track a problem. Chapters 3, 4, 5, and 6 take you deeper into specific problem areas.

Proper maintenance can reduce repair costs dramatically. Chapter 7 tells you how to reduce problems and costs by prevention. After you've read this chapter, you'll know what to do and what not to do. Knowing how to do many of the little tasks to keep your computer happy and healthy can save you a great deal of time, expense, and frustration.

Unless you know ahead of time exactly what you need in a computer system (in which case, you're a rare individual), there will come a time when you want to add something to your computer. It might be a second printer, a phone modem, or additional memory. Whatever you care to add, you'll find the help you need in Chapter 8.

*Williams: How to Repair & Maintain Your Apple Computer (Chilton)*

By following the steps in Chapter 2, you'll have a good idea of what the malfunction is, whether or not you handle the job yourself. This knowledge helps reduce repair costs and greatly decreases the risk of being ripped off by unnecessary repairs. Chapter 9 gives you some tips on dealing with the technician.

Even if you have no background in electronics, you can still handle most repairs and maintenance. However, the more you know, the easier it will be. Check with your local library for books on basic and advanced electronics. The less you know now, the more important it becomes that you pick up such books and learn a bit about electronics. Your goal is not to become an electronics whiz, just to have a more thorough understanding of what is going wrong inside your computer and why.

It is suggested that you read the entire book before tearing into your computer. Even those sections you don't think you'll need are important, because they will help give you an overall picture of the workings of your computer. Don't be in so much of a hurry that you end up causing more problems.

Before you start yanking out parts or devices, go through Chapter 2 (diagnosis) carefully. Imagine that something has gone wrong and the computer will not accept programs. If you just tear into the machine without thought, you could spend hours trying to find out what is wrong, and you may not find the problem at all. Proper diagnosis will guide you to the source of the malfunction. If the problem is with the drives, why spend time with the random-access memory (RAM)? The few minutes you spend with this chapter can save you hours of wasted effort.

Once you're familiar with Chapter 2, you can go to the appropriate chapter for further details. For example, if diagnosis indicates that the problem is with the disk drives, turn to Chapter 4. If the problem seems to be with the power supply, go to Chapter 6.

Chapter 10 is devoted to the IIc. Problems specific to this computer are discussed, and diagnostic tips are offered. Then in Chapter 11, you will learn how to use the diagnostics diskette that can be purchased with this book. Each test on the diskette is discussed individually and explained thoroughly. Finally, at the back of the book is a glossary of important terms.

Use this book correctly and it should save you at least 10 times its cost for the first repair. Instead of spending that 1% per month ($300 per year on a $2,500 system) or that 10% per year ($250 on the $2,500 system), you could be spending only $50 per year, or much less. Why spend more than you have to?

Expenses aren't in money alone. The time involved may be quite costly: time spent waiting for the technician to come or time wasted in driving to and from the shop. Then there is downtime, when your valuable computer is useless. You bought your computer to save time. Why use up what you've saved in waiting hours or days only to find out that you could have fixed the trouble yourself in a few seconds?

An added benefit is that you will understand your system better. You'll know what can go wrong. You'll learn how to fix the most common problems, and even how to prevent troubles.

## TOOLS YOU'LL NEED

The Apple is a highly sophisticated machine. It is also extremely well designed. The more you work with it, the more obvious this will become. The design allows you to troubleshoot and repair your computer with nothing more than a few basic tools. You bought several of them when you bought your computer. The main tool is the computer itself. The DOS and System Master programs will go a long way to show where the problem is. The diagnostics diskette that comes with this book takes care of virtually all other major malfunctions. If you bought the book without the diskette, you can purchase one separately. With the book as a guide, you have just about everything you need.

### REQUIRED TOOLS

Unlike so many machines of "modern" manufacture, the Apple rarely requires a special or expensive tool for repair. Chances are you already have all the tools you need. If you don't, the cash outlay to equip yourself will be small.

1. Screwdrivers—Using nothing more than a standard screwdriver and a small-headed Phillips (with insulated handles to protect yourself), you can just about completely disassemble your Apple. The keyboard is attached with screws; the mother board is held with screws; the drives are held together by screws. There is very little in the computer that doesn't come apart with a tug of the fingers or a twist of an ordinary screwdriver.

2. Multimeter—To test for voltages, to measure component values, and to check for continuity, you will need a fair-quality multimeter, or VOM. It doesn't have to be a fancy digital multimeter. A VOM costing less than $20 is fine. Voltages measured will be in the 5- and 12-volt-DC (direct current) ranges and 120 volts AC (alternating current). It should also be capable of measuring resistance (in ohms). Accuracy is important, especially in measuring voltages. If you're not familiar with using a multimeter, practice before probing inside the computer. For example, take readings of the various outlets in your home to measure AC voltage, and check some batteries for DC voltage. If you have some old resistors lying around, check those for correct resistance. It doesn't take long to learn how to use a multimeter efficiently and accurately.

*Williams: How to Repair & Maintain Your Apple Computer (Chilton)*

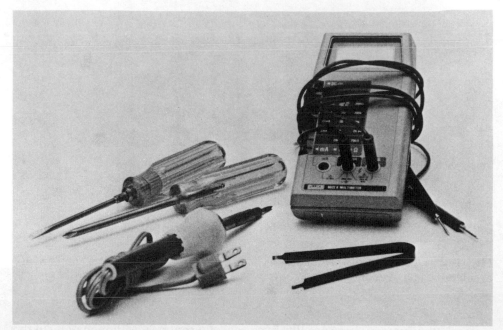

**FIG. I–1**   Required tools: screwdrivers, multimeter, soldering tool, and IC extractor.

    3. Digital soldering tool—If you intend to replace single components, you will need a high-quality soldering gun, one designed specifically for digital circuits. (If you will not be replacing components, you won't need this tool. And you can put off the investment—about $50—until you need it.) The tool should have a rating of no higher than 40 watts. If possible, the tip should be grounded to avoid electrical damage to delicate components.

    4. IC extractor—Many of the integrated circuits (ICs) in your computer are plugged into sockets. Replacing an IC is simple, risky only if you try to use your fingers alone, in which case, the many prongs of the IC are easily damaged. Thus, an extractor should be used to remove the chip from its socket safely.

## OPTIONAL TOOLS

With the two screwdrivers and the multimeter, you'll be able to take care of almost any problem and add-on. The soldering gun and IC tools will be used only if you intend to handle detailed repairs or additions. Other tools, such as those listed below, are merely to make the job easier.

    1. Needlenose pliers—You'll rarely need regular pliers. However, having a needlenose at hand makes retrieving dropped parts easier. A needlenose also helps remove parts that are being desoldered.

*Williams: How to Repair & Maintain Your Apple Computer (Chilton)*

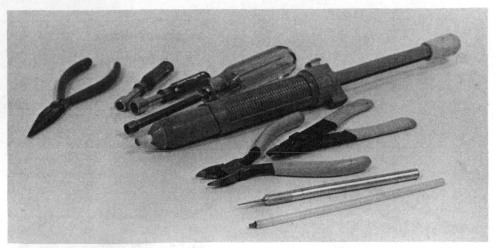

**FIG. I–2** Optional tools—to make the job easier: needlenose pliers, nut drivers, desoldering tool, wire cutters, and knife.

2. Nut drivers—These are like fixed socket wrenches. Although none of the screws on the computer have hex heads, the screws on some peripherals can be removed and installed with either the screwdriver or a hex nut driver. Quite often, a nut driver makes removal and replacement of the screws easier, faster, and safer. You won't need nut drivers for working on the computer itself, but they are often handy for working on certain peripherals, such as printers.

3. Desoldering tool—This is a fancy name for a heat-resistant syringe. Its function is to suck away solder from a heated joint. Without it, removing components is difficult and sometimes impossible.

4. Wire cutter—New components often have metal leads that are too long. This means that they must be clipped to the proper length. A wire clipper handles this job correctly and efficiently. Some pliers have built-in clippers. These are suitable for cutting wire but are not meant to trim the leads of components that are soldered in place.

5. Knife—A small, sharp knife can be used for many jobs. Used correctly, it can be a valuable tool.

Table I-1 lists required and optional tools. "RS" denotes that the part is available at Radio Shack at a competitive price. You may also find that an assembled tool kit, such as the one available from Heath Company (part number GHP-1270, $39.95), will suit your needs.

*Williams: How to Repair & Maintain Your Apple Computer (Chilton)*

**TABLE I-1**
**Required and Optional Tools**

| Part | Part Number | Approximate Cost ($) |
|------|-------------|----------------------|
| Screwdriver (blade) | any | 2.50–6.00 |
| Screwdriver (Phillips) | any | 2.50–6.00 |
| Multimeter (VOM) | 22-201 (RS) | 19.95 |
| Soldering tool (Weller) | TC201 & TC202 | 79.95 |
| IC extractor/installer | 276-1574 (RS) | 6.95 |
| Needlenose pliers | any | 5.00–10.00 |
| Nut drivers | 64-1800 (RS) | 4.99 |
| Desoldering tool | 64-2085 (RS) | 8.79 |
| Wire cutter | 64-1841 (RS) | 3.79 |
| Knife | any | varies |
| Cleaner | 64-2322 (RS) | 1.99 |

**Note:** Most of the tools do not have to be specifically for electronics. For example, the screwdriver or pliers you use to work on the car will do just fine (as long as it is clean).

# Best Results/
# Minimal Time
# 1

Have you ever watched a child take apart a toy? The usual way is for the pieces to go flying in all directions, without any order or planning. Parts that don't come off easily are broken off. Some roll under the couch; others get stepped on; some just disappear.

When it comes to reassembling the toy, the child rarely has the slightest idea of what to do or how to do it. That's when the child brings it to mommy or daddy with big, sad, wet eyes and says, "My toy broke. Fix it for me."

A fair number of computer repair jobs are a direct result of an adult "child" getting inside his electronic "toy" to find out how it works or to attempt to repair a malfunction. Quite often, what started out as a minor problem turns into something expensive.

Sure, you can save hundreds of dollars per year by doing your own repairs and maintenance and by installing any add-on equipment yourself. Approach it incorrectly, however, and it can end up costing you many times what the repair should have cost—sometimes in ways you didn't expect.

## YOUR SAFETY

Nothing is more important than your safety. If you do something that destroys a circuit in the computer, you can replace the circuit. If you let something happen to you—well, there are no such things as replacement parts.

*Williams: How to Repair & Maintain Your Apple Computer (Chilton)*

There are actually very few danger spots in your computer. Even while the computer is in operation, the voltage inside (past the power supply) is either 5 volts DC or 12 volts DC. The amount of current flowing is so tiny that you wouldn't even feel it.

The DC power used in the operation of most digital circuits isn't at all dangerous to a person. However, there are certain places where the voltage and current aren't quite so safe. These spots are usually where AC power comes into the system. Touch one of these places and you're in for a bad time.

## EFFECTS OF CURRENT

The line coming into the power supply of your computer, and into most peripherals, is 120 volts AC. The amperage can be as high as the physical limits of the wire and the circuit breaker or fuse. Usually this means that the line is 120 volts with a steady current of at least 15 amps, plus a surge limit in the hundreds of amps. This is enough power to melt a metal rod and more than enough to kill a person.

Tests were done by the U.S. Navy to learn the effects of alternating current with a frequency of 60 cycles per second (cps). (The measure of frequency is sometimes made in hertz, with one hertz equaling one cps.) It was found that a tiny trickle of just 1 milliamp (.001 amp, or one one-thousandth of an amp) produces a shock that can be felt. A current of 10 milliamps (.01 amp, or one one-hundredth of an amp) causes the muscles to become paralyzed, making it impossible for the person to let go of the source of the shock. In fact, the spasms caused by this amount of current can cause the person the grip the source more tightly. At 100 milliamps (.1 amp, or one-tenth of an amp), the shock is usually fatal if it continues for more than a second.

As you can see, it doesn't take much current to bring on a severe hazard. If you carelessly touch a hot spot, you will become a part of the power circuit. For a short time (until the fuse or circuit breaker pops) the current flows unhampered. You risk having a surge of perhaps 100 amps, which is more than 1,000 times as much as is needed to be fatal, flow through your body.

### DANGER SPOTS

Anywhere that an alternating current is present there is a risk to you. Most of these spots are obvious and easy to avoid. The danger begins with the wall outlet (or the circuit box if you fool around there). It moves up through the wires and into the power switches.

The way the wires are connected to the equipment makes it very difficult

---

## THE MOST DANGEROUS SPOTS

1. Wall outlet
2. Power cord
3. Power switches
4. Filter capacitor
5. Printers and mechanical parts
6. Monitor

---

to touch the contacts. The power supply is sealed and has a sticker on top, warning you to STAY OUT! The power supply is one of the only real electrical dangers to you inside the computer. However, there is rarely a need to open the power supply; repair is generally handled by replacing the entire unit. The average person should not attempt to get inside.

Past the switch and inside the power supply is the filter capacitor, which looks like a small can. When the alternating current enters the power supply, it is changed in value to the 5 volts or 12 volts needed. It is also changed from alternating current to direct current. The filter capacitor helps smooth out the flow by storing up current as it comes in and then letting it flow out again in a steady stream.

Even after the computer is shut off, and even with the power cord pulled from the outlet, this capacitor can have a hefty charge inside. Theoretically it should drain itself of all charge in seconds. Normally there is no danger. But you won't know if something has gone wrong with the circuitry until you touch the capacitor contacts—at which point, you'll find out all too quickly.

In the Apple and most peripherals, power goes directly to the switches. It's a common misconception that a switch is safe when it is in the off position. It is not safe unless the power cord has been removed from the outlet. If you happen to touch the incoming contacts, it would be the same as if you grabbed the bare power lines.

Some peripherals have fuses. With the switch off, there may still be current flowing through the fuse or into the device. The fuse is for protection of the circuits inside, not for your protection. If a short circuit is present, the power supply will begin to draw large amounts of current. In a very short time, this increased flow will cause serious damage. It could cause a fire. The fuse helps prevent such damage.

If the fuse is rated at 2 amps, this simply means that when the current

*Williams: How to Repair & Maintain Your Apple Computer (Chilton)*

BEST RESULTS/MINIMAL TIME

reaches a higher level, the fuse wire will melt and current will not flow beyond the fuse. For a fraction of a second, more current *can* flow, however. Worse, if you create a short circuit across the fuse, the fuse will do nothing at all. Your body, the screwdriver, or whatever is around becomes the new fuse. Generally, this means that you're grabbing a bare wire with 120 volts and temporarily unlimited current.

With the power switched to off, you can usually safely change the fuse and other power-handling components inside the power supply. (The power supply of the Apple does not have a fuse. However, many other power supplies, such as those for peripherals, do.) This again assumes that the switch is operating correctly and that the wires are all connected as they should be. Before you begin, take a moment to get out the multimeter and measure if there is voltage present.

The monitor is another source of high voltage. DO NOT open the video monitor until it has been allowed to sit overnight with the switch off. Remember that 120 volts AC enter the monitor and present the risks already discussed. In addition, there is always the chance that your monitor was wired improperly. Recently, several thousand monitors were manufactured and shipped with the wiring connected backwards. But the danger doesn't stop here.

The monitor is a cathode ray tube (CRT) that works by throwing electrons at the phosphor-coated screen. This requires a considerable charge. The larger the monitor is, the larger the voltage required to form an image. Even a small black and white monitor may require a few thousand volts. Color monitors require still more, sometimes as much as 25,000 volts. The current (amperage) is low, but this doesn't make the monitor safe.

The monitor brings yet another danger, one that has nothing to do with electricity. The screen tube has a vacuum inside and thin glass walls. Striking the tube can cause an implosion which results in sharp slivers of glass being thrown around.

## MEASURING VOLTAGE

Although most equipment manufacturers do their best to reduce the risks of accidents, you still have to be careful. Remember the case when thousands of monitors were shipped with the wires connected in the wrong order. A "hot" (active) wire was connected to a spot that should have been "dead." A technician who assumes that everything is as it should be could be in for a shock—literally.

If you are going to be working on the main lines coming into a piece of equipment, on the power switches, or on any component where an alternating

*Williams: How to Repair & Maintain Your Apple Computer (Chilton)*

**FIG. 1–1**   Learn how to use a multimeter.

current might be present, don't assume that the spot or contact is dead just because it is supposed to be. Unplug the equipment and then measure the voltage. This rule applies whenever you're working around something electrical.

Testing for "hot" is easy to learn. With a multimeter or other testing device, touch one probe (usually black) to a known ground, such as the metal chassis of the power supply. Be sure to hold the probe by the insulated handle only. Touch the other probe (usually red) to the suspected point. Assuming that the meter is functioning properly and that you've put it into the proper testing range, it will measure the charge if one is present.

Setting the meter to the correct range is important. If you intend to measure the voltage at the monitor screen, don't set the meter for 3 volts. (The setting should be in the thousands of volts. See the manual that came with your monitor.) If you're testing for alternating current, don't adjust the meter for direct current. You're asking for trouble if you jam the probes inside the computer without first looking to see if the meter is properly set.

*Williams: How to Repair & Maintain Your Apple Computer (Chilton)*

---

## PERSONAL SAFETY RULES

1. Use special, high-voltage probes only.
2. Don't touch conductive surfaces.
3. Observe the one-hand rule.
4. Use only insulated tools.
5. Beware of jewelry, hair, neckties, loose clothing.
6. Don't obstruct moving parts.

---

## SAFETY RULES

Working around electricity demands a set of safety rules. The first step is to shut off the power. The main switch will cut the flow to parts farther in. Turning off the switch doesn't protect you completely, though, since the wires between the switch and the wall outlet are still hot.

You might think that the best way to protect yourself completely would be to unplug the computer. This is true, with reservations. While pulling the plug removes the current coming in from the wall outlet, it also removes the safety of a ground wire. This step is more to prevent damage to the computer than to yourself. Whether you unplug the computer or not depends on the circumstances.

With or without the plug, assume that all circuits are live and carry a potentially dangerous current. (The vast majority do not, but if you treat them as if they do, you are unlikely to damage either the computer or yourself.)

You can't see electricity, nor can you tell by sight if a circuit is hot. The only immediate indication of power flowing inside the computer is the light on the keyboard and the soft hum of the fan (if you've installed one), which is easy to ignore once you become accustomed to it. (The IIe also has a light-emitting diode [LED] on the mother board, but this is inside the computer chassis.)

By measuring voltage, you ensure that you're not sticking your fingers in dangerous places—dangerous to you or to the computer. Use only special, high-voltage probes to read voltage.

Never probe or poke inside the computer with any part of your body touching a conductive surface. Avoid leaning on the chassis, a metal workbench, or anything made of metal when you are reaching inside. Also take care that your feet aren't touching anything conductive (which includes a damp floor). In short, insulate yourself from your surroundings and from the equipment.

*Williams: How to Repair & Maintain Your Apple Computer (Chilton)*

To further protect yourself, use the one-hand rule. This means, simply, don't reach in with both hands at the same time. Keep one hand in a pocket to avoid the temptation of breaking the rule. If one hand is in a pocket, you almost have to consciously remove it to reach inside the machine.

The idea behind this rule to is prevent your body from becoming a part of a circuit. If only one hand touches a hot spot and your body is insulated from all conductive surroundings, the current has nowhere to go. If a second hand touches a hot spot, the current can enter the first hand and pass through your body and out the other hand.

All tools should have insulated handles. Touch the tools only by these handles. It's sometimes tempting to grab a part of the blade of a screwdriver for better control, for example. Don't do it! The insulation is on the handle for a reason.

You may realize that grabbing a tool by the metal is foolish and then forget that the necklace you are wearing is made of metal. It will conduct current just as well as the shaft of a screwdriver—better if it's made of gold or silver. The same caution applies to other jewelry, such as rings. These won't be as likely to fall onto a dangerous spot, but they can touch it and carry the current into your body.

A dangling necklace might also become entangled in a mechanical part and cause problems. Inside the computer the only moving part is the fan for cooling the computer, if you've installed this. You're unlikely to catch something in this. Peripherals are another matter. Printers in particular are loaded with moving parts. Most have a tag inside warning you to remove jewelry and to be careful of long hair. (Having it yanked out by an angry printer is no way to get a haircut.)

There is no such thing as being too safe. Just when you think you've taken every possible precaution, look for something you may have forgotten.

## COMPUTER SAFETY

Once you've taken the necessary precautions to protect yourself, you can begin to think about the well-being of the computer. As with personal safety, computer safety is basically a matter of common sense. Rules such as "Don't punt the computer across the room no matter how angry you get" and "Don't resort to your hunting rifle just because you're losing at Pac-Man" should be obvious, although you'd be surprised at some of the things people have done to their computers. Other don'ts are just as obvious if you take a moment to think them out.

*Williams: How to Repair & Maintain Your Apple Computer (Chilton)*

---

## COMPUTER SAFETY RULES

1. Shut off power.
2. Take notes; make sketches.
3. Don't be in a hurry.
4. Never force anything.
5. Use the proper tools.
6. Avoid short circuits.
7. Check for screws, etc.
8. Beware of static.

---

In certain ways the computer is a surprisingly tough piece of machinery. If it operates for the first week or so, it's unlikely that anything major will go wrong for many, many years—unless you cause it. Even if you make some mistakes in operating or repairing the computer, chances are you won't do too much damage.

This doesn't mean that you are free to be careless. Just as you assume that all circuits are holding deadly charges, assume that any mistake will cause the immediate destruction of a $1,000 circuit. (It is possible.)

Again, there is no such thing as being too careful.

## PHYSICAL DAMAGE

The most common damage done by the home technician is physical. Physical damage is also the least necessary. There is no reason or excuse for it. By hurrying, losing patience, or being careless, you do the wrong thing at the wrong time and something snaps.

Most parts of the computer are tough. Others can be damaged easily. Caution is the key at all times, no matter how tough you think something is.

When removing a board, use slow and steady pressure (see Figure 1-2). The boards are supposed to be tight to maintain a reliable contact. However, they're not in so tight that they require the strength of both arms and a foot. If a board doesn't move, there is usually a logical reason. Never force anything. Take the few extra seconds to find out why the board or component won't move easily.

One computer operator decided that the boards were too difficult to remove. He took the probe of his voltmeter and jammed it into the slots of the

*Williams: How to Repair & Maintain Your Apple Computer (Chilton)*

**FIG. 1–2**   To remove an expansion board, grasp it firmly on both ends and lift.

receiving board to widen them. Then he was amazed that the operation of the computer was sporadic, at best. He ended up having to replace those receptacles—at a premium cost.

The components inside your computer have anywhere between 2 and 60 connectors. Each of these leads is prone to physical damage, mostly from bending it too far. The ICs are particularly sensitive.

The ICs, or chips, have a number of metal prongs coming from them. More often than not, the prongs on a new IC are not positioned for easy installation. Bending them manually is the usual solution for the computer owner who is installing chips. This brings in the danger of bending the prongs too much or too little and then rebending to compensate. Because of the thinness of the prongs, this bending and rebending creates stress on the metal. The prong may break off or crystallize in such a way that the current flow changes, rendering a good chip useless.

*Williams: How to Repair & Maintain Your Apple Computer (Chilton)*

### PREVENTING PHYSICAL DAMAGE

The solution to this and related problems is to use the proper tools for the job at hand. Two special tools are available to handle the delicate chips. An IC installer can be used to position the prongs correctly for installation; an IC extractor (see Figures 1-3 and 1-4) is designed to aid in the removal of chips. Both tools are fairly expensive for someone who plans to install or remove just one chip per decade. Both are inexpensive when you consider the cost per ruined chip. If you want to reduce costs, at least get an IC extractor.

These tools offer an additional safeguard. Some of the chips in the Apple are extremely sensitive to static. Your body has the tendency to store up static charges. You have probably experienced a tiny shock when touching a door-knob or other metal object after walking across a rug. If the charge was enough for you to feel it, it was probably enough to fry the insides of a delicate chip. A static charge you cannot feel may still be enough to ruin a chip.

The IC extracting and installing tools will help prevent this from happening. You can reduce static buildup by treating the carpets, either with a commercial product or with a dilute mixture of water and standard fabric softener. You can also use a static discharge device. This is a device connected to a ground (such as a neutral screw on a wall outlet). You touch a metallic spot on the device with your finger, and any static charge in your body is drained off safely.

**FIG. 1-3** IC extractor.

*Williams: How to Repair & Maintain Your Apple Computer (Chilton)*

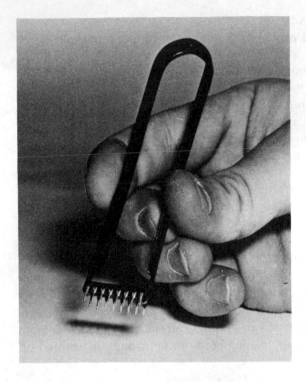

**FIG. 1–4** The prongs of an IC are delicate, and the inside can be ruined by static. Handle with care: use an IC extractor for removal.

## ELECTRICAL DAMAGE: SHORT CIRCUITS AND OHM'S LAW

The second most common type of damage caused during repair is electrical: short circuits. These can happen in several different ways.

The usual way is by touching the metal tip of a tool or probe across two points that are not meant to be connected. Usually this won't matter. Other times it will send a circuit off into oblivion with a cloud of smoke.

There is a mathematical relationship between voltage, amperage, and resistance. Ohm's Law defines this relationship: $E = I \times R$, where $E$ = voltage, $I$ = current in amps, and $R$ = resistance in ohms. If you multiply the current and the resistance, you'll know the voltage.

With some basic algebra you find that $R = E/I$ and $I = E/R$. By sticking some numbers into that last formula, you can see what happens with a short circuit.

The voltage remains constant because of the design of the power supply. In most circuits this will be 5 volts. If the resistance is 10,000 ohms, the current flowing is .0005 amps. A short circuit effectively drops this resistance to near zero, which means that the current will flow to the limit allowed by the power supply (about 2.5 amps). For computer circuits designed to handle just fractions of a milliamp, the effect can be disastrous—like trying to instantly force a few hundred gallons of water through a tiny hose meant to carry just a few ounces.

In the previous section, there was mention of necklaces and other jewelry causing current to flow into your body. While you are working inside the computer itself (outside the power supply), there isn't enough current flow to harm you. However, the rule about jewelry applies—this time to protect the computer.

The human body normally has a very high resistance. Unless your hands are wet, touching an active circuit (i.e., a digital circuit, not a circuit that carries high voltage or alternating current) is unlikely to cause any damage. A ring on your finger or a watch on your wrist is another matter. The metal will act as if you had connected a wire from spot to spot. If a necklace swings down and creates an electronic bridge, you may not be able to feel the effect, but the computer probably will. Resistance drops to near zero. As a result, current swings in the other direction.

Being careful of jewelry is easy. Other things more difficult to notice can also cause shorts.

When taking things apart, keep careful track of the various screws, bolts, nuts, and other metallic parts. Take notes, and make drawings if you think they are needed. It's all too easy for a part to fall inside the computer unnoticed, only to cause trouble later on. When you turn on the power, that lost and forgotten chunk of threaded metal becomes a surprisingly efficient conductor.

It is less likely, but still possible, that small pieces of metal may fall inside the computer. The average computer owner won't have to worry about this unless a screw has been forced (in which case, a piece of the thread may become stripped off) or the lead of a component has broken off.

### PREVENTING ELECTRICAL DAMAGE

To prevent accidental short circuits, flip the switch to cut off the power before you remove anything. There is only one reason for the power to be on while you're working inside the computer: for testing, probing, and measuring, all of which must be done carefully. For anything else, the power should be off. Make shutting down the power your automatic response and applying power what you stop and think about.

Imagine yourself working inside the computer for a simple repair, such as replacing a faulty IC. You forget the rule and leave the power on. First you pull the memory board and there is a soft "zzzt." You're being careful and use an IC extractor, but you touch the edges of the metal tool to active circuits ("zzzt,

*Williams: How to Repair & Maintain Your Apple Computer (Chilton)*

zzzt, zzzt"). You pull the faulty chip and install the new one. You've been careful about reinstallation and know that everything is where it is supposed to be. But nothing works. Each of the boards, including the one for the memory, has ruined components. You scratch your head and say, "Now how could that have happened?"

This isn't likely to happen. What is important is that it *could* happen. If a board or component is removed while current is flowing through it, the current value often changes. As the value changes in one place, other changes will occur elsewhere. Small changes probably won't cause damage although they can cause the circuit to age. Larger, sudden changes have an effect similar to that of short circuits or static discharge, namely, to destroy the circuit from the inside.

When working inside the computer (with the power off), pay attention to what you are doing. Look carefully at any connector you are going to remove. Make notes and sketches so that you have something for future reference. Before you turn the power on again, look around inside. Are all the connectors back in their proper places? Have you left any screws, nuts, or bits of metal inside? Are the accessory boards pushed all the way into their slots?

## COMPONENT REPLACEMENT

Most of the time, a component failure is handled by replacing an entire board. Even professional technicians use this method of repair. Although board replacement may sound expensive, the time involved in tracking down a problem to a single component often ends up costing more than a new board. (Don't forget that the malfunctioning board probably has a trade-in value. A board that cost $300 won't (or shouldn't) cost $300 to replace.)

Since you probably do not have the equipment that the technician has, or the knowledge to use it, you will probably confine most repairs to board replacement rather than component replacement.

Sometimes you will be able to identify the specific component and will decide to replace that piece only. When such identification is possible, the saving to you is large. Most of the components in your computer cost very little. Diodes, resistors, and capacitors cost pennies, ICs often just a few dollars. Many of the ICs used in the computer can be purchased for less than a dollar.

The first step in component replacement is to make certain that the new component is exactly the same as the one it replaces. If you're uncertain about which parts are which or how to read the component values, consult a book on basic electronics.

Some components have polarity. An electrolytic capacitor, such as the filter capacitor in the power supply, has positive and negative leads. Install a new one backwards and it could explode. Other components won't react so violently but could cause damage throughout a circuit, expensive damage. ICs that are installed incorrectly may burn up and take a whole string of other components and circuits with them.

Even when you aren't replacing a component, pay attention to polarity. For many repairs, you'll be disconnecting cables and other wires. Most of these have special keyed plugs, making it impossible to reconnect them incorrectly. You may run into a few that don't have this intelligent design, however.

Taking notes and making sketches are important parts of any repair. Get into the habit, even when you don't think that you'll need the notes and drawings. There is no need to be a professional artist or writer. What you do is primarily for your own use, a jog to your memory. Assume, though, that others will be using your notes. It's possible that you'll have to consult a professional on the repair. The notes you take and the drawings you make could save you quite a bit of time and money, regardless of how amateurish they may be.

## SOLDERING

Some components plug into place. Most are soldered into place. Despite what you might think, soldering is an art. It's not a skill you can learn in a few minutes. With circuits as critical as those of a computer, you certainly shouldn't practice soldering inside your computer. Numerous books and pamphlets on how to solder are available. Heath offers a course on soldering. Before you even consider soldering inside the computer, learn everything you can about the technique. Then practice, practice, practice.

The soldering iron used for digital circuits (see Figure 1-5), such as those in the Apple, should be rated at no more than 30 to 40 watts. Anything hotter could easily damage the circuit or the board. Even with a low-powered iron, more than a few seconds of contact is risky. Many components are very heat sensitive; the internal goodies may be fried all too easily. The board may also be damaged permanently. If this happens, you may as well scrap the board and buy a new one.

The soldering iron should be designed specially for digital soldering. These irons are more expensive, but they are worth the extra cost. They have grounded tips, which prevent damage from any buildup of electrical charge. Don't try to use any ol' soldering iron or gun for the job.

To remove a component, especially one with many contacts (such as an IC), be sure to use a desoldering tool. This inexpensive device removes the melted solder from the contacts, making it possible simply to pull the old component

*Williams: How to Repair & Maintain Your Apple Computer (Chilton)*

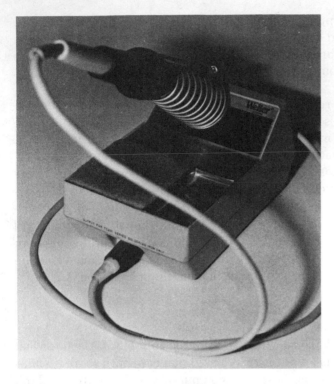

**FIG. 1–5**  A soldering tool for digital circuits.

loose. Move slowly and carefully so as not to cause damage. The more contacts the component has, the trickier it is to remove it.

## PREPARING TO WORK

Before you begin any repair, you should have a solid understanding of the correct procedure. Diagnosis and repair consist of a logical sequence of steps. (More on this in Chapter 2.) Learn these steps. Follow them. They'll save you money, time, frustration, and a whole lot of trouble.

The first step is so simple that most people ignore it. Make backups of every bit of software. Many books and courses suggest making a copy. Instead, make at least two copies. Having the original plus the two copies helps protect you.

If you don't know how to make a copy, refer to your DOS manual. (This routine is on the System Master diskette.) After copying, perform an accuracy test. Run each copy to be sure that it works properly or that it contains the correct data. Always test at the time of making the copy. If you don't, you won't know for certain if your copy *is* a copy or just a useless diskette.

*Williams: How to Repair & Maintain Your Apple Computer (Chilton)*

---

## PROTECT YOURSELF

1. Make at least two backups.
2. Test the backups.
3. Store the original and one backup safely.

---

Losses occur through fire, water, forgetfulness, and so forth. These possibilities should always be of concern to you, however unlikely they might seem. You must also consider loss through the machine.

In a very large computer repair house, a certain technician fed in a diagnostics diskette. There was a problem with the disk drive. The result was that the machine "ate" the diskette. His solution was to feed in a second diskette. The computer destroyed that one as well. So he booted up a third, then a fourth. By the time he figured out that the drive was annihilating the recorded programs, five copies were destroyed.

This may sound silly. A professional should know better. The typical operator may not. If the problem is intermittent, it would be very easy for even the most experienced operator to waste a program or two before realizing what the problem is.

If your machine doesn't accept the original, try a copy. If the copy doesn't work, chances are something is wrong with the machine. If the problem has erased the first two, you have the third to protect yourself.

## WHERE IS THE PROBLEM?

Computers are extraordinarily reliable. Most people blame machines when something goes wrong. In many cases the machine is at fault. A car that suddenly stalls on the freeway usually exhibits a machine error. A television or radio that refuses to work usually displays a fault in the equipment. With a computer, the fault is often with the person running it.

Most common machines are designed so that anyone can operate them. There aren't many variables for the operator to change. A television, for example, has very few controls. The owner can switch it on, change the channel, and adjust the contrast and color within limitations. Beyond this, about all the television operator does is sit back and view.

Operating a computer usually involves pushing various buttons, each of which performs a different task. It's like having thousands of controls available

*Williams: How to Repair & Maintain Your Apple Computer (Chilton)*

---

## IMPORTANT QUESTIONS TO ASK YOURSELF

1. Has the program ever worked?
2. Has that function of the program ever worked?
3. Do other programs work?
4. What is working, and what is not?

*Where Is the Fault?*
1. Operator
2. Software
3. Peripherals
4. Disk drives
5. Computer

---

instead of just a half dozen. Just as the computer offers more controls, it brings many more opportunities for making mistakes.

Before you tear into your computer, make sure that the fault lies with the computer. Chances are good that the fault lies with you or the programmer: most malfunctions are not the fault of the computer.

One of the first questions you should ask yourself is, "Has the program ever worked?" An untried program may have flaws. Even a known program may have bugs in it. A tried-and-true program may give out after a number of uses. (Diskettes are well manufactured but aren't without error; nor do they last forever.) Then there are those programs with functions you use every day but also with other capabilities you haven't yet used. When you get around to trying those, you're back to a "Has it ever worked?" situation.

Your first suspicion should be with yourself (or the computer operator). Software documentation is notorious for being poorly written. Do you (or does the operator) understand how to work the program? Have you read the instruction manual thoroughly? Are you trying a new function of the same program?

Second in the line of things to suspect should come the software itself. If you have backup copies, try one of these. If you have been using the program successfully and have tested the copies for all functions, you can eliminate the "Has it ever worked?" question.

Another test is to boot up a different program. For example, if your word processing program isn't working, try your accounting program or one of the games you have. You can use the System Master diskette if you happen to have only one working program. Of course, you should have working copies of all important software, which can be used to test the loading.

If you have checked out any possible operator and software failure, the next step is the visual check. Look for what doesn't look right. Don't start pulling boards and components until you've completed this step. Look for the obvious. Much of the time you can solve the problem with very little effort.

*Williams: How to Repair & Maintain Your Apple Computer (Chilton)*

Perhaps you've dropped a screw or nut and this is shorting one of the internal circuits. Maybe the door to the disk drive is cracked and won't allow the spindle to make proper contact with the diskette (an unfortunately common problem).

It is also possible that the problem is being caused by an incompatible board, a protection scheme on the program, or a combination of both. A friend of mine has a modem card installed. Certain programs cannot be loaded unless he removes this card. This is because a special protection scheme used on those programs causes the computer to look for a different kind of board where the modem is.

Another possible cause is again the result of protection schemes. Some half-height drives read and write strictly 48 tracks per inch (TPI). One protection scheme puts certain information halfway between the tracks. The half-height drive may be incapable of seeking the information here, which in turn means that the program won't load.

The next step is to use a diagnostics diskette. If you bought this book with the accompanying diskette, you're all set. (Chapter 11 tells you how to use the diskette.) If you bought the book separately, you can purchase one of several commercially available diskettes.

Notes should be taken throughout the diagnostic process. Even before you put in the diagnostics diskette, you should have something written down. What is working. What is not? Jot down all the symptoms along with any error signals that the computer kicks out. As the diagnostics program is being run, continue to take notes.

Don't waste your time on parts that are functioning properly; diagnosis is a process of elimination. If you know that the drives are accepting programs, that your printer is operating, and that the monitor is giving a correct image for what is being sent to it, then eliminate these parts of the computer. If the problem is that the RAM won't hold data, why waste time taking apart the drive? Probably, all you'll do is cause more problems.

Begin with the most obvious and the easiest. Work your way to the more complex.

All checks begin with the cabinet closed. Check and recheck for operator error—then for software error or for diskette failure. Only then should you think about opening the cabinet. And you should have at least a fair idea of what you're looking for before opening the cabinet.

When you do open the cabinet, move slowly and deliberately. With the box open, look for the obvious. All you can cause is damage if you're in too much of a hurry.

*Williams: How to Repair & Maintain Your Apple Computer (Chilton)*

---

### ENEMIES

1. Dust                    5. Other contaminants
2. Liquid                  6. Humidity
3. Food                    7. Weight or pressure
4. Smoke                   8. Carelessness (i.e., you)

---

## PREVENTING PROBLEMS

Chapter 7 deals with maintenance. Your Apple has been designed and built to require very little maintenance. You can pretty much ignore your machine, and it will keep going.

There are still some TLC requirements.

The greatest enemy of the computer is dust. A tiny fleck of dust that your eye can't even see can gouge a diskette to uselessness. Dust combined with humidity can cause short circuits. Yet dust is everywhere. All you can really do is reduce the amount that gets into your computer, particularly into the mechanical parts. Some dust on the boards is unlikely to cause any problems. However, just a few invisible particles on the disk drive heads can slice the data on a diskette to shreds.

Keep the area around the computer as clean as possible. DO NOT use a feather duster or anything similar. A slightly damp rag will pick up dust rather than toss it into the air, where it will do even more damage. Store all diskettes safely, both inside their jackets and inside a diskette storage box.

One problem you can eliminate entirely is food and drink. Make it a policy never to allow anything spillable within a 20-foot radius of the computer. If you or another operator wants a cup of coffee, it's time for a break *away* from the computer.

Liquids in particular are dangerous. Spilled into the keyboard, they can cause damage that necessitates replacement of the keyboard and can create short circuits that lead to other repairs.

## SUMMARY

A computer is a logical machine. Things don't go wrong for no reason. Just because you can't see it right away doesn't mean that the reason isn't there.

The do's and don'ts are little more than common sense put to practice. If

*Williams: How to Repair & Maintain Your Apple Computer (Chilton)*

## PROCEDURE

1. Read the book thoroughly.
2. Read Chapter 1 again for safety tips.
3. Perform diagnosis (Chapter 2).
4. Read applicable repair chapter (3–6).
5. Repair or replace.
6. Consult a professional if needed.
7. Back in operation again!

something seems silly, don't do it. If it seems logical and sensible, think it over before you do it. Don't attempt to do anything unless you have some idea of what you are doing and how to do it. Likewise, don't attempt a repair without the proper equipment. To put it even more simply, "When in doubt, *don't.*"

In making repairs, keep in mind that the design of the machine demands exact components. If a resistor goes out, the replacement must have exactly the same value.

Suspect yourself first. Next, suspect the software and diskettes. Begin all checks with the cabinet still closed. Take notes frequently and make sketches when applicable. Don't trust your memory.

Finally, read through the entire applicable chapter before you attempt to work on a section of your computer. If you suspect the drives, for example, read Chapters 3 and 4 thoroughly before you begin. (Read Chapter 2 thoroughly before you do anything!)

Repair and maintenance of a computer are not all that formidable. People less intelligent than you are doing it every day without making errors. At the same time, people more intelligent are messing things up faster than they can be repaired, almost always because they refuse to follow "the rules."

*Williams: How to Repair & Maintain Your Apple Computer (Chilton)*

====================================

# Diagnosis: What's Wrong with It?
# 2

When something goes wrong with your computer, it's tempting to remove the cover immediately and start poking around. Even if you have some idea as to what has happened (or has not happened), this is probably the worst way to begin. The cure of a problem *always* begins with the cabinet closed and usually with the power off.

Some problems can be solved immediately, in less time than it takes to call in and wait for a repairperson. Others may take more time. You'll learn which problems to tackle yourself and which to save for a technician.

Diagnosis is a step-by-step process. The primary steps are covered in this chapter. Once you have used these steps to track a problem to a particular system or device, you will be guided to the appropriate section of the book for further diagnosis and for the final repair or replacement.

For example, imagine that your computer refuses to accept a program. The potential causes are many. This chapter will take you through a diagnosis until you have tracked the problem to a single part of the computer system. If the problem is in the software, you would then turn to Chapter 3 for more details. If the preliminary diagnosis indicates that the problem is caused by the disk drives, you would go to Chapter 4.

It's as simple as that. When a problem comes up, begin right here in this chapter (unless you already know for sure what is causing the problem). This chapter will help you eliminate many of the things that are not causing the problem. You can then more easily pin down what is malfunctioning.

*Williams: How to Repair & Maintain Your Apple Computer (Chilton)*

Throughout the diagnostic process, take a lot of notes. What is happening? What is not happening? What symptoms are you noticing? If you have to take the computer to a technician later on, these notes will save you time and money. Even if you perform the repair yourself, the notes will help guide you along and will also serve for future reference.

The notes should include sketches. This way you'll have an easier time reassembling things after you're finished. Don't trust your memory. It's too easy to forget that screw number 17 fits into slot number four to hold two particular components together.

The Apple's plugs and connectors are keyed. (This may not be true for certain devices from other manufacturers.) Even so, keep track of which connector goes where. The more you disassemble, the more important the notes and sketches.

## FIRST STEPS

Most problems and malfunctions can be taken care of without ever taking the computer apart. Many can be spotted and cured without even turning on the power.

The diagnostic process consists of eight steps:
1. Check for operator error.
2. Check for software error.
3. Look for the obvious.
4. Observe symptoms.
5. Use the diagnostics diskette.
6. Run the built-in self-test (IIe).
7. Repair or replace when you can.
8. Consult a technician when you can't, armed with all the above information to save time and money.

Remember to take notes and make sketches throughout these steps.

## CHECK FOR OPERATOR ERROR

A computer has remarkably few hardware malfunctions. Despite its appearance, the computer is relatively simple—much less complex than, for example, your television set. If something goes wrong with the television set, chances are the fault lies in the set. After all, there is little opportunity for operator error. There aren't many knobs to adjust, or misadjust, and the only "programming" is provided by the local broadcasting companies. Even the new programmable television sets require little on the part of the operator.

*Williams: How to Repair & Maintain Your Apple Computer (Chilton)*

In contrast, the computer works because of what the operator does. It has hundreds of controls, generally accessed through the keyboard. The more controls you are required to operate, the more likely you are to mess up somewhere along the way.

If you, the technician, are also the operator, much of the time you'll know when you make a mistake. If the operator is someone other than yourself, this may not be true. It's possible that as an operator tries to recover from an error, the problem could get worse, making your job of tracking it down more difficult.

Your first BASIC programs are excellent examples of how important operator error can be. Each command has to be just right. A program directs the computer through a complex electronic maze. Give it incorrect directions and the computer will get "lost."

Don't think that operator error can occur only with "home-brew" programs. Even software that has been professionally written and produced isn't free of suspicion. (See the next section.) A flawless program can present some very strange problems if you don't understand its functions, characteristics, and quirks.

Does the operator know how to operate the program? Is it a new program or perhaps a new feature of a familiar program? If either is true—if the program or function has never worked—then it's possible that the "malfunction" is nothing more than a lack of knowledge on the part of the operator.

If you were to spend some time in a computer repair shop and listen to some of the malfunctions (and their solutions), you'd realize just how many things the operator can do wrong. It has nothing to do with being stupid or even careless. Most of the time, the problem results from a simple mistake. One operator was never shown how to start the machine, let alone how to run it after it was going. Another had the power cord kicked out by the family dog and couldn't figure out why the computer seemed dead. Still another erased a large amount of valuable data because he thought that the diskettes had to go through INIT each time before they could be loaded.

If there's even the remotest possibility that the problem is operator error, check it out completely before blaming the computer. Of all computer "malfunctions," about a third are brought about by nothing more than operator error.

## CHECK FOR SOFTWARE ERROR

Once you've eliminated the operator as the source of the error, be sure that the software isn't the cause. This includes both the data on the diskettes and the diskettes themselves. Both can produce errors that may seem to be machine problems. Of all problems that come into a repair shop, the vast majority are brought on either by operator error or by software error. In a sense, the software becomes a sort of operator once it's fed into the computer. It tells the computer what to do and how to do it when the human operator pushes the various keys.

New programs and diskettes are especially suspect. Just because the box and plastic wrapper are intact doesn't mean that the diskette is flawless. In some ways, diskettes are as delicate as Christmas tree bulbs. (See Chapter 3.) Despite all the care and testing, a flaw might have sneaked in during manufacture. Or the diskette might have been damaged in transit.

A program or section of a program on the diskette might have been imperfect to begin with. (I have a chess game in which the king cheats whenever he is in trouble.) Newer programs are more open to suspicion than programs that have been around for a long time. After several thousand users run the program and find the errors, the manufacturer can release an improved version. (That new programs often contain weaknesses of various sorts isn't necessarily the fault of the manufacturer, although it is likely.)

Making backup copies of all software and data diskettes protects you from software failure. You should have at least one backup copy of anything that is important to you. Two copies are better yet. Be sure to test the copy before storing it. Then if something goes wrong with the original, you'll have a quick means of recovery. You'll also have a way to test to see if the problem is in the software or the hardware.

## LOOK FOR THE OBVIOUS

A new computer owner took his system home and pushed in the program diskette (just as he'd been shown at the shop), but nothing happened. That same afternoon he tucked all the equipment in his car and brought it back in. It operated flawlessly, so he took it back home again, only to have the system refuse to operate again. The next day he was back in the shop.

"I just don't understand it," he said. "I know the outlet is good because I plugged a lamp into it. Maybe something got jiggled inside the computer when it was in the car." Again the system operated perfectly in the shop, with the owner watching. Then he saw the technician reach back to flip off the power. "What's that black switch for?" he asked.

That may sound silly, but it is a true story. Somehow the customer managed to get the idea that shoving in the disk automatically kicked in the power. It's such an obvious thing that the salesperson hadn't even bothered to show the customer how to apply power to the computer.

*Williams: How to Repair & Maintain Your Apple Computer (Chilton)*

This customer might have been tempted to rip off the cabinet to see what was the matter. It probably would have done no harm. On the other hand, he could have caused damage before he realized that all he had to do was flip a switch.

Look for the obvious before you do anything else. If the computer seems dead, look to see if the plug is still in the outlet, and check to make sure that the power switch has been flipped before you tear apart the power supply.

The same applies to all cables and connectors. It's easy for them to become loose even if your computer sits perfectly still. You can't always tell if the connector is secure just by looking, either. Push them in to make sure that contact is being made.

Contrast and other controls on the monitor may be bumped or accidentally turned so that something seems to be wrong. The more people who touch your system, the greater the chance that something has been bumped, nudged, or otherwise messed up by human action.

If a program refuses to load, the reason could be as simple as having accidentally inserted the disk upside down or even having put in the wrong diskette. A flickering on the screen or a recording error could be caused by someone in the next room turning on a vacuum cleaner or an electric mixer.

Then there are physical-construction problems due to normal wear and tear. What appears to be a major problem with a disk drive may be nothing more than a broken door. (They're plastic and all too breakable.)

Even inside the computer keep your eyes open for the obvious. There are more connectors inside the cabinet. The boards may not have been pushed all the way into the expansion slots. A screw may have fallen to cause a short. Components are sometimes obviously damaged. A capacitor might be leaking fluid, or a resistor might be obviously burned. A soldered connection might be loose.

Not quite so obvious is a problem caused by an incompatible board, a protection scheme on the program, the way a particular drive works, or a combination of these. If a board is incompatible, it can keep certain or all programs from loading. It can also cause the computer to malfunction in other ways or even prevent the computer from operating at all. Some boards require a particular slot, but a program might be looking for something else in that slot. This problem can keep some programs from loading.

Some drives, especially half-height drives, read and write strictly 48 TPI. One protection scheme (designed to foil software pirates) puts certain information halfway between the tracks, which in a sense forces the drive to be a 96 TPI drive. If your drive is incapable of seeking the data stored on these "tracks between the tracks," your problem may appear serious while in fact it may be nothing more than a slight incompatibility.

*Williams: How to Repair & Maintain Your Apple Computer (Chilton)*

As you're going through the more detailed steps of diagnosis, keep looking for the obvious. Start with the simple, obvious things and then go to the more complex.

### CHECK FOR POWER

If all connections seem sound and still nothing happens, it's time to check the incoming power. Checking for power in an outlet is easy: plug something else, such as a lamp, into the socket. If the lamp lights, you know that there is power coming in through the outlet. It won't tell you much more than this, though.

Using a meter is a more accurate gauge (see Figure 2–1. Set the meter to read in the 120-volt-AC range.) It will tell you not only if power is coming in but also how much. Power companies are famous for producing "dirty" power (i.e., power with periodic drops and surges). The problem is compounded during times of peak power demand. In the middle of a hot summer afternoon, for example, the power company may be having a hard time keeping up with the demand placed on the lines by thousands of air conditioners. Line voltage is bound to drop.

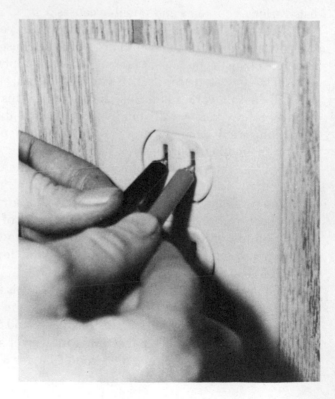

**FIG. 2–1** Using a meter to check for power.

*Williams: How to Repair & Maintain Your Apple Computer (Chilton)*

The power supply in the Apple will easily tolerate any voltage between 107 and 132 volts. If the voltage goes beyond these limits, a built-in safety circuit will shut everything down. Even below the computer's 107-volt minimum, a lamp will probably work fine. The lamp seems to indicate that the outlet is good, yet the computer will still refuse to function. Using a meter to check the outlet voltage is more certain.

If you have a fan installed, this is an automatic clue. It is wired directly to the incoming 120-volt line. If the fan is running, the outlet and power cable are good, and the problem is probably in the power supply.

## OBSERVE SYMPTOMS

If there is a problem, it will usually show up as soon as you apply power. Observe how the computer comes on while everything is functioning properly.

The normal sequence is for the light on the keyboard to indicate power, followed by a beep, followed by the prompt on the monitor. If a disk drive is attached, the LED on its front panel should come on, indicating that the drive is at least trying to load the diskette.

A variation in this sequence could be caused by many things. Table 2-1 lists various symptoms and possible causes.

If nothing happens when you apply power, you would probably suspect the power supply. This may or may not be the cause. You can find out quickly. After checking the outlet and making sure it is supplying the correct AC voltage, shut off the power, disconnect all external devices, and then apply power again. If it still doesn't work, again shut off the power. This time open the case (Figure 2-2). Carefully remove all internal boards and disconnect the keyboard. If everything is still dead, the problem is either in the power supply (go to Chapter 6) or in the mother board (go to Chapter 5).

If power returns, the problem either is in one of the devices or is a weak power supply. This can be determined by reinstalling each of the devices, one at a time (with the power off each time). When power fails again, you'll know which board or device to suspect. Remove some of the boards that seemed to be working in order to reduce the load on the power supply. Install the suspected board and apply power again. If power flows, the power supply is at fault. If it doesn't, the board or device is at fault.

One problem, especially with the II and II+, is a screen filled with random characters. Usually if this happens, the light on the keyboard turns on, but the computer won't give the normal, healthy beep, and the disk drive will not start up. These symptoms indicate that either the power supply or the mother board is faulty. Follow the steps above or go to Chapter 6 for information on how to

TABLE 2-1
Computer Symptoms and Possible Causes

| Symptom | Possible Problem | Cure | Chapter |
|---|---|---|---|
| Light on keyboard does not come on | Light bulb bad | Replace bulb | 6 |
| | No power | Check obvious | |
| | | Check power supply | 6 |
| | Keyboard cable bad | Replace cable | 6 |
| | Keyboard bad | Replace keyboard | 6 |
| | Mother board bad | Replace mother board | 5 |
| Bell does not beep | Speaker bad | Replace speaker | |
| | Mother board bad | Replace mother board | 5 |
| No display | Monitor not turned on | Turn monitor on | 6 |
| | No signal to monitor | Check cables | 6 |
| | No power to monitor | Check power | 6 |
| | Monitor bad | Check monitor | 6 |
| | Mother board bad | Replace mother board | 5 |
| Drive LED does not come on | LED bad | Check LED | 4 |
| | No power to drives | Check power | 4,6 |
| | Disk drive bad | Check disk drive | 4 |
| | Drive controller card bad | Replace card | 4 |
| | Mother board bad | Replace mother board | 5 |
| Keyboard does not work | Keyboard not plugged in | Plug in keyboard | |
| | Keyboard bad | Check keyboard | 6 |
| | Keyboard cable bad | Test cable | 6 |
| | Mother board bad | Replace mother board | 5 |
| Programs cannot be loaded | Drive door broken | Check for obvious | |
| | Diskette bad | Try backup | |
| | Wrong DOS version | Change DOS | |
| | Drive not working | Check with diagnostics diskette | |
| | | Check drive | 4 |
| | | Replace drive | |
| | Drive cable bad | Check drive cable | 4 |
| | Memory bad | Check with diagnostics diskette | |
| | | Replace if necessary | 5,6 |
| | Mother board bad | Replace mother board | 5 |
| Colors are wrong | Monitor or TV out of adjustment | Adjust monitor | 6 |
| | Mother board bad | Replace mother board | 5 |

*Williams: How to Repair & Maintain Your Apple Computer (Chilton)*

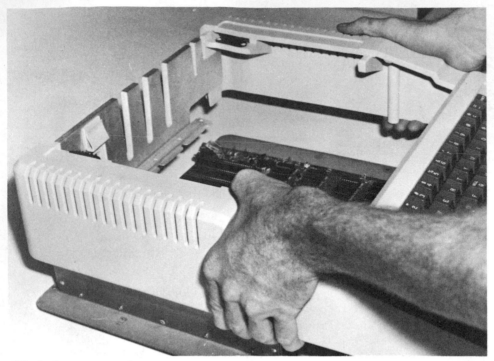

**FIG. 2-2**   Opening the case.

check the power supply. If the power supply has been eliminated as the cause, see Chapter 5 for more information on the mother board. The fault is most likely either the 74LS74 power reset chip, the 14.318MHz crystal, or one or more of the three 8T97 chips. (The IIe does not have the 74LS74 for power reset.) One of these problems is likely only when all four symptoms, which are easily noticeable, occur—when the keyboard light goes on, the screen displays junk characters, the bell doesn't ring, and the disk drive doesn't start. (See the "Normal Response" section of this chapter.)

## USE THE DIAGNOSTICS DISKETTE

Although you can diagnose many malfunctions with nothing more than your eyes and common sense, a diagnostics diskette makes the job much easier. The purpose of such a diskette is to help you spot most problems and run periodic checks. By using a diskette and the information contained in this chapter, you'll be able to track most of the common failures within your system—often down to the individual components.

*Williams: How to Repair & Maintain Your Apple Computer (Chilton)*

A variety of diagnostics programs are available for the Apple computers. If you bought this book as part of a package, you'll already have the diskette.

This diskette can save you many frustrating hours. Why waste hours trying to determine the problem when you have the tool to do so right in front of you— your computer? Most machines lack the ability to tell you what's wrong. Your computer has this ability; you must learn how to use it.

The diagnostics routines on the diskette aren't just for finding problems after they've happened. The diskette should be used regularly to keep track of how things are inside the computer. It should also be used whenever you've made any change in the system, moved the system, or left it idle for an extended period of time.

Chapter 11 contains complete instructions on how to use the routines.

## RUN THE BUILT-IN SELF-TEST (IIe)

The Apple IIe has a built-in self-test. You can get it to work by pressing CONTROL, SOLID APPLE, and RESET simultaneously. A simple, quick check of the RAM, peripheral slots, and input/output (I/O) of the computer is then performed. The self-test will not check external devices attached to the Apple. With a fully loaded IIe, the check takes just a few seconds. For more information on the self-test, see your reference manual and Appendix B of this book.

## NORMAL RESPONSE

When the computer is turned on, the screen will have junk on it. It will clear, a beep will follow, and the computer will show one of several different things.

The old Apple II with read-only memory (ROM) that does not have auto-start will show the asterisk (*) prompt on the monitor. A ROM card installed in slot 0 will probably have autostart and will cause the computer to simulate the newer Apple II+. The newer Apple IIs with an autostart ROM will start up with the greater-than (>) prompt of Integer BASIC unless an Applesoft ROM card with an autostart ROM has been installed. Again, the computer will act like the II+. If the ROM card was selected (there was a small toggle switch in back allowing you to select the ROM chips on the mother board or those on the card), the computer will use the chips on the card. Otherwise, it will use the ones on the mother board.

The bracket (]) prompt will appear only if you have selected an Applesoft ROM card or if a RAM card is in a computer using Integer BASIC and the HELLO program selects Applesoft. If a machine has Integer BASIC ROM chips, it will boot up to a greater-than (>) prompt. In other words, the computer will boot up to Applesoft or Integer BASIC depending on which is selected.

*Williams: How to Repair & Maintain Your Apple Computer (Chilton)*

One utility available with Integer BASIC is called a miniassembler. It has an exclamation point (!) prompt. It is not available in Applesoft mode.

If a drive card is attached, the computer will try to boot a diskette. The II+ and IIe will start up with the bracket (]) prompt of Applesoft. If a drive card is in, the computer will also try to boot the diskette.

If a diskette is not in the drive, if the drive is malfunctioning, or if the computer booting the diskette does not have as much memory as the one that initialized the diskette (you probably don't need to worry about this because almost every Apple has 48K bytes in it now), the disk drive will continue to spin, and the LED will stay lighted.

This will also happen if you try to boot up a disk with the wrong DOS on it—for example, if a 16-sector machine tries to boot up a 13-sector disk. The next step in this case is to try to boot up a different diskette and check with the catalog on the first diskette. This should tell you if the allocations are incorrect. You can also try to use BOOT13 on the II and II+, or START13 on the IIe. Both are on the System Master diskette for your computer. If you are using a different operating system, such as Pascal or CP/M, boot up the master and try to get information, such as a catalog, from the first diskette.

## SUMMARY

Diagnosis is a matter of listing the possible causes and then eliminating those that are not responsible until you find the one or two things that are causing problems. This is not nearly as difficult as it sounds. You already have all the tools you'll need.

Most problems have nothing to do with the computer or its devices. By careful observation, you should be able to find out if the malfunction is with the operator (most common trouble), the software (second most common trouble), or the computer.

The computer will usually tell you exactly what is wrong and where. The symptoms will indicate what is causing trouble. From there it is a process of elimination until the cause has been found.

If you have a diagnostics diskette, go through all the testing procedures provided on the diskette while your system is operating correctly so that you will know what things are supposed to look like.

Anytime something seems to be malfunctioning, take notes. Make drawings if you do any disassembly. Both will guide you along and will provide valuable information for any technicians you may need to consult.

*Williams: How to Repair & Maintain Your Apple Computer (Chilton)*

==

# Diskettes and Software
# 3

If you were to tell a repair technician that your computer was malfunctioning and that the problem wasn't something obvious like a power supply failure, he or she would immediately try to find out two things. First, what was the operator doing at the time? Second, is the software functioning, and has it ever functioned?

Operator error occurs for many reasons. Even the most experienced operator can make a mistake now and then. The more complex the program is, the more likely it is that the fault is with the operator. Before you write a nasty letter to the software or hardware manufacturer, eliminate all possibility of operator error. (Don't be too surprised if you find that the fault is yours even if you're sure it isn't.)

Ask yourself, "What have I done wrong?" Then ask, "Has the software ever worked?" Don't answer either too quickly. After all, would you rather spend hours disassembling a machine or a few seconds being honest with yourself?

Go through the manual and other documentation again. These materials are notorious for being poorly written. (I know several people who have erased $500 programs because of confusing instructions in the installation sections of the manuals.) Many manuals have an index, which can help you find the information you need on a particular subject quickly, even though the information may be scattered throughout the manual.

*Williams: How to Repair & Maintain Your Apple Computer (Chilton)*

New programs are always suspect, both for software and operator error. If you've never used the program before, you may not be putting in the proper commands. (Back to that lousy manual again.) Or you may be using a feature of the program for the first time. (Back to the manual.)

All clear? The fault is definitely not yours but with the diskette? Fine. Now we can proceed.

## DISKETTES

The usual method of data input and storage with the Apple Series II models is by using $5\frac{1}{4}$-inch diskettes. These are often called *floppies* because of their flexible nature and are sometimes simply called media. If you think about what diskettes are and what they do, it might seem strange that they don't cause more problems.

Information is packed onto the surface of the diskette. Each byte—that is, a character or other piece of data that contains eight pulses—takes up little more than a ten-thousandth of a square inch. (The space used to store a byte is about a hundredth of an inch wide and a few thousandths of an inch long.) Just as your Apple won't accept a DOS command with a character missing, it probably won't accept a diskette with a scratch or blockage over a critical spot, even if the damage is less than a thousandth of an inch in any direction.

Diskettes are the least expensive part of your system. They are also one of the most critical. Try to save by buying cheap or poor-quality diskettes and you take the chance of losing in a larger sense. Although an unknown brand may be of equal quality with "big name" brands, you are generally better off dealing with a respected brand, at least for critical programs and data.

## HOW DISKETTES ARE MADE

The diskette begins as a thin sheet of flexible plastic. Mylar is the standard. (The generic name for the material is polyethylene terephthalate.) The plastic comes to the disk manufacturer in rolls that are about a foot wide and often about a mile long. The rolls are tested, inspected, and cleaned.

Next the plastic is given a magnetic coating on both sides, even if the diskette is later given the "single sided" label. This coating is made up of extremely fine magnetic particles, a binder (like glue), and a lubricant. The microscopic particles have to be "glued" to make a uniform coating across the surface of the plastic. If they are not, there will be gaps, and data will not be accurately recorded or read.

Once coated, the plastic is smoothed and placed back on a roll, and then each roll is given a number for identification. It is then stamped into the disk shape and polished (burnished). The rougher the surface is, the more damage it will do to the diskette read/write heads. (The lubricant also reduces head wear.) It isn't possible to prevent all wear, but better manufacturers use various means to reduce wear as much as possible.

The finished diskettes are placed inside the square outer covering, which is usually made of polyvinyl chloride (PVC) plastic. Inside this jacket is a layer of thin, soft material that helps keep the surface of the diskette clean. Without this layer, the diskette would constantly be attacking the read/write head with particles of dust and other contaminants. The liner helps protect the read/write heads by gently cleaning contaminants away. It also protects the diskette surface by preventing the diskette from rubbing against the harder plastic jacket. (See the "Storage" section of this chapter.)

Throughout the manufacture of the diskette, tests are run. Its final label (single sided, double sided, single density, double density, quadruple density, etc.) is determined by these tests. A diskette that passes all the tests is given the highest rating, and the highest cost. The more tests the diskette fails, the lower its rating and its price.

What this means in simple terms is that the less-expensive diskettes (single sided, single density) have the same basic surface and manufacture as the more-expensive ones. They've just failed some highly sophisticated test along the way, and the manufacturer doesn't want to guarantee that they will accurately hold data in higher densities. It's a fairly common practice for computer owners to try to save money by buying the less-expensive, single-sided diskettes and using them as double-sided ones. (This doesn't matter to the Apple owner, of course, because the drives are single sided.)

## ANATOMY OF A DISKETTE

The computer's formatting program (INIT on the System Master diskette) divides the diskette into the correct number of sectors and sets the size of those sectors. A diskette formatted by an IBM, for example, will simply not work in the Apple, unless you put that diskette through the formatting routine for your own computer. This routine destroys all data stored on the diskette, so DO NOT attempt to format a diskette that has on it data you wish to save.

There are two basic disk types. A hard-sector disk or diskette has a series of index holes to mark the sectors. These are preset by the manufacturer. Such diskettes are typically good only for certain machines. A soft-sector diskette has a single index hole to mark the first sector, after which all other sectors are marked magnetically.

*Williams: How to Repair & Maintain Your Apple Computer (Chilton)*

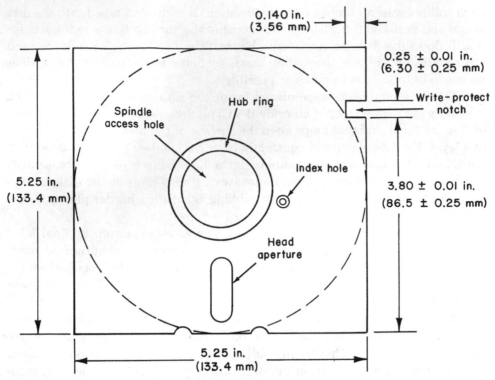

**FIG. 3-1** Anatomy of a diskette.

Since the Apple doesn't use the index hole, it doesn't matter if the diskette was manufactured as hard sector or soft sector. The computer assigns those sectors in the data section of the diskette (i.e., the oblong hole where the data is stored).

For the Apple, there are 35 tracks (numbered 0 through 34). These are like the grooves of a record, except that they are concentric circles and not in a spiral. When you hear your disk drive grind, it is because the read/write head is moving from track to track. (The sound you hear is the head stepper motor causing the read/write head to move. For more information on this, see Chapter 4.) Standard track width is about a hundredth of an inch, with normal density being about 6,000 bits per linear inch.

Each track is divided into 16 sectors (13 sectors for DOS 3.2), with each sector capable of holding 256 bytes of data. Each track, then, can hold 4,096 bytes of information (3,328 bytes for a 13-sector track). One side of a diskette can hold 143,360 bytes (35 tracks × 16 sectors × 256 bytes). To make things easier, this is called 140K. (Under DOS 3.2, each side can hold $35 \times 13 \times 256$, or 116,480 bytes.)

In the center of the diskette is a round hole about an inch in diameter. This allows the spindle in the drive to make contact with the diskette and spin it. Most diskettes also have a band of extra material called a hub ring, placed around the spindle access hole (see Figure 3-1). This ring both protects the diskette from damage by adding strength where it is needed most and allows a better contact between diskette and spindle.

Very close to the spindle access hole is the small index access hole. As discussed earlier, the Apple does not use it.

The oblong cut from the diskette cover allows the read/write head of the drive to get at the information. This is the most sensitive part of the entire diskette. A fingerprint here can cause all sorts of troubles, both to the data (including format information) and to the read/write head in the drive.

When putting new labels on the diskettes, be sure to keep the read/write access hole open and uncovered. If it is covered, two things will happen. First, the diskette won't work. The machine will give an I/O ERROR. To the computer, there is nothing in the drive. Second and worse, the glue from the label may come off onto the recording surface of the diskette. If this happens, you may as well trash the diskette. You cannot clean a diskette, nor should you try.

Along the side of most diskettes is the write-protect notch (see Figure 3-1), which allows a switch inside the drive (see Chapter 4) to activate the recording head. When this notch is covered with tape, the recording head cannot function, and you cannot write information onto the diskette. (You can read from the diskette, however. It's a good idea to cover this notch on any diskette that contains data you won't be changing.)

You can get or make diskettes that have a write-protect notch on both sides of the diskette. Such diskettes will also have a second index hole. When these extra notches are present, the diskette is usually called a *flippy floppy*, which means that you can use the diskette as though it were two single-sided floppies. To make use of the second side, all you have to do is turn the diskette over. The second write-protect notch will allow the drive to look at the second side of the diskette as a new one.

A flippy floppy allows you to use all 280K of storage available on the diskette. You can have a program of up to 140K on each side, complete with a HELLO function that allows the program to boot up by itself. The primary advantage is convenience. Usually a flippy floppy costs about twice as much as a regular single-sided diskette.

A flippy has the disadvantage that it tends to wear out sooner. As it is used on one side, it rotates in one direction. When you flip it over, rotation is in the opposite direction. This causes wear and may also increase the possibility of scratches on the surface from particles captured by the lining.

Some people physically cut a read/write notch into the diskette, thereby saving the added cost of buying a flippy. There are two problems with this. First, the manufacturer warrants only what has been sold—that is, if the diskette was manufactured and sold as a single-sided diskette, the second side is not guaranteed to retain data. (In fact, cutting in the notch voids the warranty on both sides.)

Second and more important, the jacket of the diskette is usually made of PVC plastic. This stuff has the unfortunate tendency to shatter rather than to cut. If the notch isn't cut just right, tiny flakes of PVC will contaminate the diskette and possibly the disk drive.

### HOW DELICATE IS A DISKETTE?

Despite its apparent complexity, the diskette is surprisingly tough. Many professional technicians tell stories of playing catch with an unjacketed diskette and then having it perform flawlessly. Diskettes that have been almost shredded by deep scratches zip through the drive as though brand new.

At the same time, a tiny piece of dust could cause a diskette to "crash" and become useless. And lost data is not the only risk. Each speck of dust may be ruining the read/write head while it is slowly grinding the magnetic coating from the diskette surface.

The disk drive of the Apple reads and writes 48 TPI, which means that the 35 tracks used for data, plus the empty spaces between the tracks, are squeezed into just $\frac{5}{6}$ of an inch. On a typical single-density drive, the 143,360 bytes per side are packed into about 6 square inches of surface area.

Now you can see why the diskettes and drives are so sensitive. The read/write heads record and retrieve information from tracks that are about a hundredth of an inch wide and separated from each other by about a hundredth of an inch—all this while the diskette is spinning merrily at about 300 rpm. If the accuracy is off by the slightest amount, or if something gets in the way, the data on the diskette may be inaccessible.

## CARE OF DISKETTES

You can't easily repair software. If your business program is malfunctioning, you won't be able to get inside to fix it. (You can fix programs that you've written yourself or that are written in a language you can use such as BASIC.) Your goal is to prevent problems before they occur.

*Williams: How to Repair & Maintain Your Apple Computer (Chilton)*

---

WARNING                                    •

If you try to make a single-sided diskette into a flippy floppy, you could damage your computer drives.

---

Software problems can be greatly reduced simply by taking care of the
diskettes. The disk is tough but not indestructible. It's also unpredictable. One
day you can play catch with the diskette and not damage it. The next day a
speck of dust or particle of cigarette smoke could fall onto the diskette and wipe
out everything. Improper diskette care not only can destroy software and stored
data but also can damage the disk drives. According to Verbatim Corporation,
at least 80% of all diskette failure is attributable to fingerprints.

Care of diskettes is neither complicated nor time-consuming. Manufacturers have taken great pains to ensure that diskettes will last for a very long time
with a minimum of problems. Extensive testing is done before diskettes are
sold. It's not uncommon for a manufacturer to guarantee that the diskette will
not fail even after several million passes per track. This translates to nearly a
year of continuous running before the diskette's life expectancy is reached.
Since normal operation calls for the diskette to be running just seconds out of
every operating hour, the disk should, and could, last a lifetime.

The life span of a diskette also varies according to how it is used. Although
the manufacturer might guarantee the diskette for 3 million passes per track,
each time you use the diskette it goes to the catalog track. Some applications
refer to this track over and over. Thus, the life of a diskette depends largely on
how many times the one track can be used. As soon as this track wears out, the
rest of the diskette is essentially dead.

The diskette can withstand any temperature between 50 and 120 degrees
Fahrenheit (10 to 50 degrees centigrade) and still operate without error,
although such extremes should be avoided. Even if the temperature goes outside this range, the diskette is still likely to recover if you give it enough time
to cool down or warm up. (See "Heat and Cold" later in the chapter.)

Humidity does little damage. The accepted range for diskette operation is
between 20% and 80% (5% to 95% for storage). Drier environments tend to dry
out the diskette (although this takes quite a while). Worse, static can build up,
causing changes in data. More humid areas may cause dust to stick to the diskette and the liner to swell. Swelling may impede diskette spinning and result
in an error display. Table 3-1 summarizes diskette specification standards.

*Williams: How to Repair & Maintain Your Apple Computer (Chilton)*

**TABLE 3–1**
**Diskette Specification Standards**

| | |
|---|---|
| Tracks per Inch | 48 |
| Tracks for Data | 35 |
| Track Width | .0108 to .0128 inch |
| Track Density | 6,000 bits per inch |
| Temperature | |
|    Operation | 50°F to 112 °F |
| | 10°C to 50°C |
|    Storage | −40°F to 140°F |
| | −40°C to 60°C |
| Humidity | |
|    Operation | 20% to 80% |
|    Storage | 5% to 95% |
| Disk Speed | 300 rpm |

### PHYSICAL DAMAGE

The soft liner inside the jacket doesn't just keep the diskette clean. It also serves as a cushion for the diskette in order to prevent damage. However, it can't protect the disk against everything. This is up to you.

Anything that puts pressure against the diskette can cause a dent in the jacket, the liner, or both. At best the diskette will have a hard time spinning in the drive. If this is all that happens, you may have enough time to make a copy of the ruined floppy.

This is why a felt-tip pen is suggested for writing on the labels. (Write on the label *before* sticking it onto the diskette.) The tip of a ball-point pen or pencil can easily damage the diskette. Even a soft felt tip can dent the diskette. The pressure you use in writing may not seem like much, but remember that all the pressure is concentrated at the tip of the pen or pencil. You are pressing down with only a few ounces of force, but the surface area of the pen tip is only a few thousandths of an inch. The force is effectively multiplied.

Weight of any kind pressing against the floppy can cause damage. Diskettes are best stored vertically. This not only protects the diskettes but also reduces the risk that you forget and drop a stack of books on top of a diskette.

The problem is further compounded if dust or other particles are trapped in the liner. Dust may seem soft. To understand what it can do, just take a look at the metal and glass parts of a car left in a dust storm.

Pretend that the soft liner of the diskette is made from sandpaper. You wouldn't risk the information stored on such a diskette by placing even small amounts of weight on it.

*Williams: How to Repair & Maintain Your Apple Computer (Chilton)*

### STORAGE

When not in use, diskettes should be stored in their cover jackets (preferably standing vertically inside a box). This is to reduce the amount of dust and other particles. The soft inner lining helps protect the read/write heads but tends to capture particles, which can scratch the diskette. With the data so tightly packed (143,360 bytes per side), even a small scratch can have devastating effects. If the scratch occurs over a critical bit of data, the rest of the diskette is useless.

A quality storage box (see Figure 3-2) may cost $30 or more. This sounds expensive until you consider what you're protecting. Many computer owners have invested thousands of hours in punching in data and hundreds of dollars in software. It's not unusual for a computer owner to have more invested in software than in the computer system itself. Why take the chance of throwing all that down the drain just to save a few dollars?

If you can't afford to buy a diskette storage box, make one. Such a box should not be made of metal (because of magnetism). Use wood or plastic, or even cardboard. The inside should be clean and unpainted (to avoid fumes). The top should close tightly enough to seal out dust. Beyond that, it can be as fancy or as simple as you wish. (I know people who use modified shoe boxes with great success.)

**FIG. 3–2** Diskette storage box.

*Williams: How to Repair & Maintain Your Apple Computer (Chilton)*

These are not good solutions, however. Wood and paper both have large amounts of dust and other small particles, no matter how well you clean them. These particles can ruin the diskettes and possibly the drive. Plastic is a much better solution, but it is more difficult to work with. By the time you've bought the plastic and built the case, you probably would have saved by just buying a premade box.

However you do it, keep dust and other particles and contaminants to a minimum. You've invested too much time and money to waste it on a poorly kept environment.

If a diskette gets dirty, DO NOT attempt to clean it. Your cleaning is virtually guaranteed to cause more damage than any amount of dust. How dirty the diskette is and what kind of contamination it has will determine what you do with it. If it isn't too bad, store it for severe emergencies. Otherwise, toss it out. A dirty diskette means that it's time to pull out one of the backups. (Make another backup before going to work.)

### MAGNETISM

The data on the diskettes is stored magnetically. It should be obvious that you have to keep the diskettes away from other sources of magnetism. Yet computer operators are constantly erasing their valuable programs and data through contact with other sources. Some cases are as blatant as setting the diskette next to the magnet of a speaker. Most involve more subtle sources of magnetism.

Inside the telephone is a small electromagnet. Normally it just sits there and does nothing. Whenever someone calls, that little device lets fly with enough magnetism to destroy a diskette. (It rings the bell in the telephone.)

Other potentially dangerous sources are the monitor, the printer, the modem, the cabinet of the computer, tape recording machines, fluorescent lights, and even calculators. Motors work by using magnetic fields. If you're not sure, don't trust it. (Anything metal is automatically suspect.)

It's unlikely that these subtle sources of magnetism will ruin a program, but why take the chance? It's easier to pay attention to the surroundings and keep the diskettes away from any possible danger.

### HEAT AND COLD

More important than solar radiation is the heat generated by the sun. Since the diskette is usually black, it tends to gather more than its share of the heat. Leaving it in the open sunlight is likely to cause damage. Even if it's too close to a normal incandescent lamp, it could pick up enough heat to cause damage.

Keep the diskettes away from all sources of heat. At best, heat can warp the diskette jacket. If this happens, the data you've recorded won't be in the same place on the diskette. It won't matter, though. If the diskette or jacket becomes warped, the diskette probably won't spin in the drive.

The same things can happen with cold. Not only can extreme cold cause the diskette to crack, but it can also cause the recorded data to shift in position. A sudden change in temperature can cause other problems as well.

Even a slight change in temperature and the resulting contraction or expansion can cause the tracks to move away from where they are supposed to be. Keep in mind that the tracks are just barely more than a hundredth of an inch wide and that each byte of data covers a mere ten-thousandth of a square inch.

## BACKUP COPIES

*Always* make backup copies of important programs (if possible) and data. The cost of diskettes is low considering their value to you. Making backups is the least expensive method there is to protect yourself against software failure. Make at least two backup copies of all software and data diskettes that are important to you. The more important the original is, the more backups you'll want to make. If you decide later that you don't need that backup copy, you can always reformat the diskettes and use them again. In the meantime, you'll be protected.

The manufacturer guarantees that the diskette will function without error for a certain period of time or for a certain number of passes. These guarantees *do not* cover the data on the diskettes, however. If a diskette goes bad, the manufacturer will replace it with a new diskette of the same kind, but the data is lost forever, as is the time you spent in punching it in.

## PROGRAM PROBLEMS

If you're writing your own programs, you're almost bound to make some mistakes. The Apple will generally tell you that you have made a mistake and will even show you the lines with mistakes.

If your program doesn't work, accuse yourself before you accuse the computer. Refer to the DOS and BASIC manuals to make sure that the commands you've punched in are correct. If you like programming, take some courses on the subject or get some books. Learn the most efficient procedures.

When it comes to purchased software, you have much less control over what has been done. Many programs are inaccessible for corrections. Unfortunately, so are all too many software companies. It isn't uncommon for a company to place on a software package a disclaimer that says in effect, "If the program doesn't function as promised—tough! You bought it; now it's your problem." Other companies support their products, but at an additional cost. (The old, "If you can't understand our poorly written manual, pay us an extra $100 and we'll explain it to you" attitude.)

At other times, you might be pleasantly surprised at the response. Some companies do everything possible to make sure that the end user is happy and satisfied with the program.

Before you contact a company about a software malfunction, make sure the error isn't your own. Read the manual carefully and thoroughly. If the problem still hasn't been solved, be as specific as possible in your communication to the company. Give the representative as many details as possible, including your attempts to correct the problem, and the version of the software you're using. An "It doesn't work. Why?" question won't bring much of a response.

Notes showing what you've done will help both you and the company representative. The more information you provide, the quicker the solution to the problem. Even jot down the page numbers in the instruction manual so you can readily refer to the appropriate section.


## FAILURE TO BOOT

There are a number of reasons why a program will fail to load. The most common reason is a bad diskette. The fault may also be with the drive, the power supply, the memory, or even the keyboard. Usually it is quite easy to find out what is causing the problem. Do one thing at a time in a process of elimination until you've located the trouble. Don't forget that the problem might be board or program incompatibility or a copy-protect scheme that is causing an apparent malfunction.

Eliminate all the obvious things first. Is there any power at all? (If the plug is secure and the outlet has been checked and there is still no power, go to "The Power Supply" in Chapter 6.)

Are you using a new program (the "Has it ever worked?" question)? Or perhaps the diskette you're using is very old and has simply worn out. Try another diskette, one that you know is good. If this one loads, you'll know that the fault lies with the software. (Use the diskette that is not critical. Although it is rare, it is possible for the drive to malfunction and write over the top of a diskette, even if it is write protected.)

It's possible that the diskette you're trying to load is too large for the memory you have in the computer. Usually this will be displayed. Sometimes it will not.

I was trying without much luck to get a particular program to load. It loaded

*Williams: How to Repair & Maintain Your Apple Computer (Chilton)*

to a certain extent but would stop, say PROGRAM TOO LARGE, and give the bracket
(]) prompt. The fault was obviously in the software since other programs loaded
without trouble. The computer being used had 48K. The program itself required
slightly less than this and should have loaded without any problem. There was
no sign that the memory was too small. The problem turned out to be with the
size of the DOS installed on the software. DOS 3.3, which requires somewhat
more RAM than the earlier versions, was used. The difference was just enough
to cause the software to fail in loading. With DOS 3.2, the program loaded and
executed perfectly.

If some disks boot and others do not, run the diagnostics diskette. (See
Chapter 11.) This should show you if the fault is with the software, the memory,
the drives, or something else. If you are unable to boot any of the diskettes you
have, try the System Master diskette. If this boots, it may tell you that the top
16K of RAM is faulty. (See Chapter 5.) The System Master will relocate the
memory for its own use. This won't help you run some programs, but you will
then know that there is a problem, and where this problem is. If the System
Master diskette refuses to boot, see Chapter 4 on disk drives.

Before disconnecting anything, look for the obvious. Is the door to the drive
intact? (The usual symptom of this problem is that the drive will continually
spin without any apparent effect.) Are the cables firmly attached to the drives
and to the drive card inside the Apple?

A simple test of the drives involves switching the cables. Remove the cable
from each drive and install them again in reverse order (i.e., the connector that
was on drive 1 gets connected to drive 2; the connector for drive 2 goes to drive
1). Obviously, you must have two drives to try a swap. For more information on
the drives, go to Chapter 4.

## OTHER PROBLEMS

There will be times when a program loads and operates normally, only to malfunction while the program is running. Data may suddenly come out changed
or missing. The program could cause the keyboard to lock, resulting in loss of
the data you've been punching in.

If the problem is in the software (in the program itself), you should be able
to reproduce the malfunction by pressing the same keys again. You may have
already noticed where the failure occurs. Notes will come in handy in tracking
down the problem.

Changed or garbled data can often be the result of overediting. The computer will automatically assign a chunk of data to a spot on the diskette. If possible, it will record these chunks in sequence. If something has been placed in

the next spot on the diskette, the data will be moved along until an open spot is found. This tends to disperse the file over the diskette. In reading such a broken file, the computer might miss something.

The solution for this is to copy files occasionally. This will help rearrange the file in sequential order. You can copy a single file, or you can use FID (FILEM on the IIe) to copy the entire diskette, with an equal sign ( = ) as a file name. It is best to use a freshly formatted diskette for the copy, since a diskette with data on it could break up the files even more (to make the data fit between existing files).

One track on the diskette is set aside for file allocation. Each time you bring up the directory of the diskette, the computer goes to this track and displays the files. Each time you tell the computer to load a program or data file, it again goes to the allocation table to find out where the needed file is.

Earlier in this chapter we talked about how many passes a diskette can withstand before it malfunctions (3 million passes per track). It seems as though the diskette could last forever. It *will* last for many years. The passes against the allocation track constitute the main source of wear. Each time the file is read, recorded, or used in any way, the drive head goes back to the allocation track. After a few years of this, the track might fail. Although the information on the rest of the diskette is still good, access is difficult because the allocation track no longer tells the computer where to look.

The track can become faulty for other reasons. Some programs do not exit "gracefully." If such a program is in use and you lose power—through a planned shutdown or an unplanned power outage—the allocation table can become messed up. The end result is about the same as if the track had worn out.

The solution for both is prevention. Make backup copies of everything important. The more you use a particular diskette, the more important backups are. If a diskette has been in use for a long time, make a copy and replace it *before* it gives out.

## SUMMARY

Most computer malfunctions are caused by either the operator or the software. Eliminating operator error is a matter of proper training and paying attention. The simplest beginning is to read the instructions. Learn how to work with the program and how to handle its functions and its quirks.

Since you are unlikely to be the author of your functional programs, you cannot eliminate software problems. If the package comes to you with flaws in it, there won't be much that you can do, other than to return the package for a refund. As soon as possible after getting a new program, test it out. The longer you wait to do this, the more difficult it will be to get a refund or an exchange.

Make backups of all important software and data diskettes. Two backup copies of each is none too few. It's an inexpensive insurance against loss through operator error, diskette flaw, or drive malfunction.

Taking care of the diskettes is simple, because there is nothing to do other than preventive steps. Provide a clean environment. Keep the diskettes away from things that could damage them, such as magnetic forces, heat, and contaminants.

Handle them properly and they can last a lifetime. When they finally wear out, you always have the backup copies to turn to.

===

# The Disk Drives
# 4

The electronics of a computer allows electrons to move through the proper components at the proper times. The only motion is that of the electrons, and virtually the only wear is that caused by the heating and cooling. Something mechanical is bound to have more troubles than something that doesn't move physically at all.

The only mechanical parts of the Apple are the fan (if you have one), the printer, and the disk drives. The keyboard is also mechanical in that it requires a physical movement to operate. Of all failures in your computer system, most will involve either the printer or the drives. (Printers are covered in Chapter 6.)

The disk drives are critical parts of the computer system. Without them, your system is severely limited. Although the Apple is set up to take a cassette, this method of storage is considerably slower, and there are fewer programs available. Most people either buy their system with at least one disk drive or upgrade later on.

## DRIVE TYPES

The Apple uses two basic drive types. Several other manufacturers make drives compatible with the Apple. Many of the steps for diagnostics and repair are the same no matter what kind of drive you have. A few things are different, but most differences are unlikely to concern you. The tests and adjustments are the same except for the diskette stop guide adjustment. Most differences show up only for some complicated tests that require an oscilloscope and specially prepared diskettes.

Before you go through the following steps, you should know which drive type you have. The name is usually printed on the bottom of the mechanical assembly. To see it, you will probably have to remove the bottom part of the drive cabinet.

Probably the most common type is the Alps Apple Disk II (see Figure 4–1). The name "Apple Computer, Inc." is on the bottom of the mechanical assembly. The other official Apple drive is made by Shugart Associates; this name will appear on the label of the drive. The BMC half-height drive (see Figure 4–2) is also widely used.

**FIG. 4–1**  Alps drive.

*Williams: How to Repair & Maintain Your Apple Computer (Chilton)*

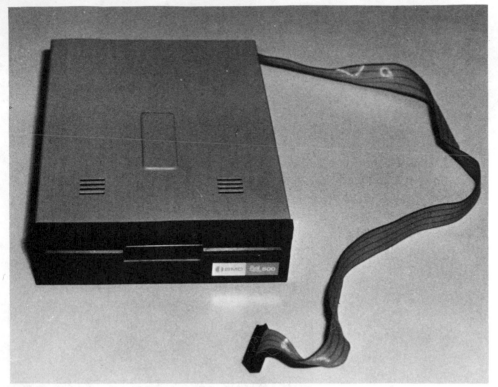

**FIG. 4–2**  BMC half-height drive.

## CHECK THE OBVIOUS

Serious malfunctions in the drive are relatively rare. Most of the problems are brought on by small things, which often have nothing to do with drive operation directly. Don't yank out the drives until you've eliminated all the easy things.

The drive door is made of plastic. It has the unfortunate tendency to break. Even if the break doesn't completely separate the door from the drive, it could still prevent the drive from functioning properly. The hub may not make a secure contact with the diskette, or the drive may simply "think" that the door hasn't been closed.

As the drive door goes down, the diskette is placed in the correct position for the spindle to make a positive contact and for the read/write heads to be close enough to do their job. If the door doesn't come down and lock into place properly, the computer is likely to see the drive as having an open door. The result is that the diskette won't spin and the program won't load. The usual

*Williams: How to Repair & Maintain Your Apple Computer (Chilton)*

procedure for a broken door in drive 1 is that the computer will wait for you to close the door, which you won't be able to do, since it is broken. The problem could also be intermittent, with data being read or recorded with errors.

Replacement of the door is simple. The door assembly is held in place by two screws located at the top front of the drive. Push down on the metal lever arm and remove the screws, as shown in Figure 4-3. The assembly should lift out easily, and the replacement should go back in just as easily. Alignment is important but not critical. Before you tighten the screws, make sure that the door closes securely, as shown in Figure 4-4.

One of the biggest problems with the drive isn't the drive at all but the software. If the software isn't operating the way it should be, it could seem that the drive is malfunctioning. (See Chapter 3.)

If you haven't cleaned the heads in some time, there could be deposits that are preventing the heads from operating. Data that is read or written incorrectly

**FIG. 4–3**   Remove the door assembly screws.

*Williams: How to Repair & Maintain Your Apple Computer (Chilton)*

**FIG. 4–4**  Make sure the door closes tightly.

or intermittently could mean that a dirty head is causing a problem. (See Chapter 7 for more information on cleaning the drive heads.)

Have you made any changes in your system? If so, you may have changed something inside the computer. If everything was working perfectly before the change, you've done something wrong in making the change.

Are the cables secure? Try unplugging them and pushing them back into place. If the contacts appear to be a little dirty, clean them. You can use either a cleaner that doesn't leave a residue (see the required and optional tools table (I–1) in the introduction) or the eraser of a pencil (taking care to keep the eraser shreds out of the computer). Be sure to shut down the power before removing or inserting any cables or circuit boards. Failure to do so will almost certainly damage the board and the computer.

For example, if the disk drive cable is shifted by one set of pins in any direction (front, back, or toward the right), damage will be done to the interface card, the drive analog card, or both. The usual result of this cable being plugged in incorrectly is for the 74LS125 IC chip on the analog card to explode violently. Usually you can repair the damage simply by replacing the chip. However, sometimes the explosion can cause other damage, such as to the analog card itself.

Other ICs may also be damaged, although these rarely explode. There might not even be any sign of damage. The analog board or interface card in the computer may just stop working. Without some very expensive test equipment, all you can do is replace some of the chips to see if this corrects the malfunction.

## PRELIMINARY STEPS

Before you go into the actual diagnostics to find out what has gone wrong with a drive, you can try several easy things.

The first step is always to observe the symptoms and then to eliminate those things that are not causing the problem. Notes are important.

If the LED on the front panel of the drive comes on, you know that power is getting to the drive. You can then eliminate the power supply as the source of the problem. You should have already checked all cable and board connections, cleaned the heads, checked the door, tried a different program (or a backup copy of the same program), and performed all other steps to check for the obvious.

Run the diagnostics diskette if you have one. The diagnostics diskette will check the drive in its various functions. (This assumes that the drive will operate and load the diskette.) Make a note of all error codes. Run the Media Verify test (on the System Master program) a number of times on a diskette that has been formatted on a good drive. This will indicate the general condition of the drive. For example, errors on many sectors could indicate that the drive is unable to read correctly. The drive may need alignment in this case. Errors could also indicate a dirty read/write head.

Next, if you have two drives, you can try a simple swap (see Figure 4-5). Open the cabinet and change the connections to the drives so that drive 2 is connected as drive 1 and vice versa. Run the diagnostics diskette again to see if the error changes. For example, if drive 1 was showing a problem before the swap and you connect drive 2 as drive 1, drive 2 should now show the error. If it does, you'll know the problem is with drive 1. If the symptoms are the same, chances are that the fault is somewhere other than the drives.

See also "The Power Supply" in Chapter 6, since a faulty drive could cause the entire system to go dead. Try using each drive as drive 1, with the drive 2 connector eliminated. Disconnect the cables from drive 2 and run the diagnos-

*Williams: How to Repair & Maintain Your Apple Computer (Chilton)*

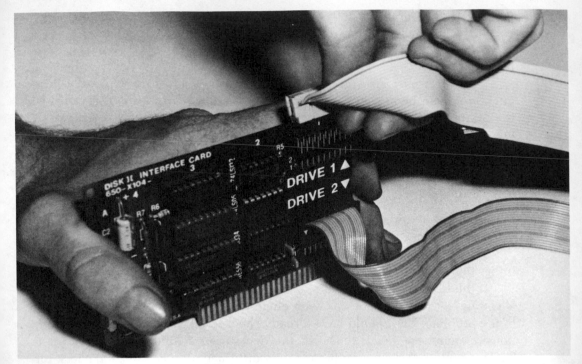

**FIG. 4–5**   Swapping the drive cables.

tics. Then switch the lines so that the second drive acts as drive 1, with the first drive disconnected. Run diagnostics again and watch for a change in the operation, in the error code, or in both.

Don't forget to take notes and make sketches. This is especially important if you are going to be disassembling anything.


## ADJUSTING THE CARRIAGE LIMITER

A common problem with Apple drives is a maladjustment of the carriage limiter. When this happens, the drive seems to be operating fine, except that it won't load properly. If this adjustment is incorrect, the drive may load sometimes and refuse to load other times.

Open the drive and remove the analog card (the board on top of the mechanism). Figure 4-6 shows the drive analog card. You'll see a large white or yellowish wheel with a groove in it. This is the carriage limiter cam, which is

**FIG. 4–6**   Drive analog card.

shown in Figure 4–7. Rotate the cam clockwise to move the head to the back of the drive. With the head at its farthest position, look at the position of the small dot on the cam. It should be just to the right of center of the cam follower—the small metal tab protruding from the rear of the cam (see Figure 4–7). If the dot is to the left of center or off to the side of the metal tab (refer to Figure 4–8), your drive needs adjustment.

To adjust the drive, unscrew the small screw (see Figure 4–9) and move the cam. Be very careful, as this movement tends to damage the screw threads all too easily. Once you have the cam adjusted, carefully tighten the screw again.

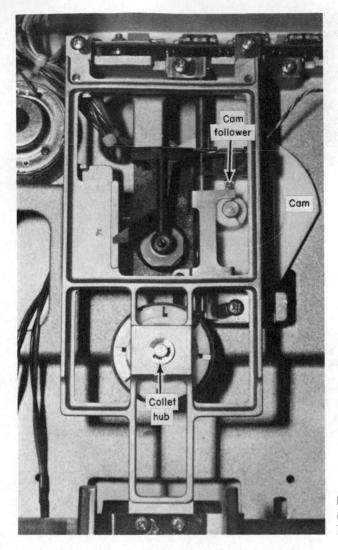

**FIG. 4–7** Carriage limiter cam, cam follower, and collet hub.

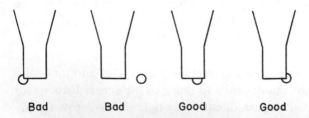

Bad          Bad          Good          Good          **FIG. 4–8** Cam dot locations.

*Williams: How to Repair & Maintain Your Apple Computer (Chilton)*

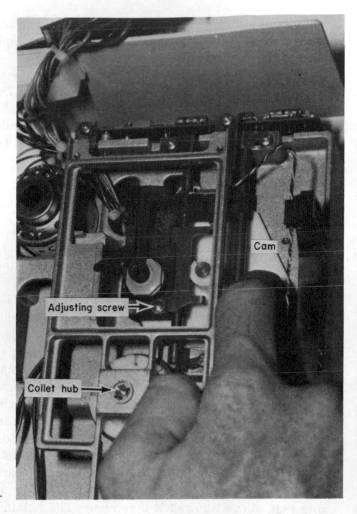

**FIG. 4-9** Adjusting screw.

## ADJUSTING THE COLLET HUB

If the carriage limiter cam is in proper adjustment and programs still won't load properly, the problem could be with the hub and spindle (see Figure 4-7). This is especially common with drives that are a few years old. A secure contact is needed if the diskette is to spin correctly. Quite often, if the hub is out of adjustment, opening and closing the door a few times reseats the spindle and allows you to load the program.

With the drive cabinet and analog card removed, look straight down at the collet spindle and close the door. The shaft should be centered. As you open and close the drive door, the hub should move cleanly and evenly in and out of the receptacle. If it does not, or if it seems to change, the mechanism may need to be adjusted.

There are four screws on the metal bracket. Two of these are at the back, with the other two holding the bracket to the door. Loosen all four screws and then close the door. The bracket can now be moved until the shaft is right in the center of the hole. Tighten the rear screws and check the alignment by opening and closing the door. With the door open, reach inside and push the shaft with your finger. If it is adjusted properly and the screws are tight, the shaft should still sit properly in the hole.

## REPLACING THE COLLET HUB

If your drive is old or has been used extensively, you might not be able to adjust the hub. Repair is by replacement. (See "Adjusting the Diskette Stop Guide" in this chapter before going to this expense.)

Remove the front panel. (If the wires to the LED are too short to allow this, refer to "Changing the Drive LED" in this chapter before continuing. The front panel must be out of the way before you can safely remove the hub assembly.) The hub assembly is held in place by a retaining clip, which can be easily removed with a screwdriver. Once the clip is no longer in the way, the assembly slides off easily. Be careful as you take out the spring and washer. If you stretch or damage the spring, the repair will be much more expensive.

When replacing the collet hub, follow the disassembly steps in reverse. The sketches you've made (you did make sketches, didn't you?) will show that the small end of the spring goes down. The hub assembly should slide easily onto the mounting arm. Replace the retaining clip carefully so as not to damage the hub or shaft. If you had to remove the LED to get off the front panel, be sure that you've reinstalled it correctly. The holding pins for the drive door should be tilted back toward the collet hub to allow easy installation. Once the front panel is in place again, adjust the collet hub assembly and drive door (see next section) carefully.

## ADJUSTING THE DRIVE DOOR

Before tightening the two front screws of the bracket, check the door for proper alignment. It should be flush with the front panel. You should be able to see if the door is crooked. As with a broken door, a drive door that is not seating correctly can cause the drive to think that it is empty.

*Williams: How to Repair & Maintain Your Apple Computer (Chilton)*

The two holding screws were loosened in the previous step. If you skipped the hub adjustment, loosen the two bracket screws on the door. The door can now be moved and adjusted so that it is flush with the panel.

Tighten the two screws. Insert a diskette and gently close the door while watching the two guide bars. (These guide bars stick straight down on the back surface of the panel.) There should be no binding between these guide bars and the diskette. If there is, the door needs further adjustment. Loosen the screws and adjust the door so that the guide bars just touch the diskette, without binding against it.

## ADJUSTING THE DISKETTE STOP GUIDE

If you still have errors after checking or adjusting the collet hub and drive door, the problem could be the diskette stop guide. When this is not adjusted properly, the collet hub and spindle cannot make proper contact with the diskette.

The diskette stop guide is a piece of plastic or metal that stops the diskette from moving in too far when the diskette is inserted into the drive. It's rare for this guide to go out of adjustment. Usually, the only time it does is if someone has tinkered with it. However, if it is far enough out of adjustment, not only will you get drive errors, but you could also permanently damage the diskettes.

The Alps drive has a stop guide that cannot be adjusted at all because it is a physical part of the mechanical assembly casting. The stop guide on a Shugart drive can be adjusted.

Remove the drive cover and analog card. With the inside now exposed, insert a diskette and gently close the door while watching to see if the diskette is centering and if the collet hub spindle is seating correctly. There should be very little movement of the diskette with the spindle clamped.

If the diskette is too far forward or back, manually place the diskette in the correct position. Loosen the mounting screw and gently move the guide until it just touches the diskette, and then tighten the screw again. If you happen to have some Gliptol or Locktite, put a little on the screw. (These liquids are used on screws to help keep them from wiggling loose.)

## REPLACING THE HEAD LOAD BUTTON

Occasional I/O errors could be the result of a worn head load button. This button is a small felt pad on the bottom of the read/write head assembly (see Figure 4-10). Its function is to push down against the diskette while the read/write head presses up from beneath. This holds the surface of the diskette flat against

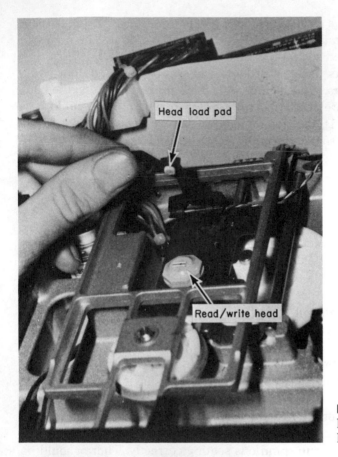

**FIG. 4–10** The read/write head assembly and the head load pad.

the head. If the pad wears, the diskette may not be held perfectly flat. Data may be lost. A heavily worn pad can also damage the diskettes. If the pad falls out (rare, but it happens), the diskette can become badly scratched or destroyed.

A worn pad will often be skewed to one side. It might also look hard and dried-out. Either way, it should be replaced.

The top of the head load pad is a plastic cylinder with a round cone on top. The cylinder and cone have a notch cut into them. The assembly is forced up into the arm and spreads apart to hold it in; thus glue is not required.

To change the pad, lift the head load arm and grasp the pad carefully with a needlenose pliers as shown in Figure 4-11. The button usually comes off easily. The new head load button gets inserted into the holder. A slight push will snap it into place.

You can usually get a head load button from your local dealer. Prices vary.

*Williams: How to Repair & Maintain Your Apple Computer (Chilton)*

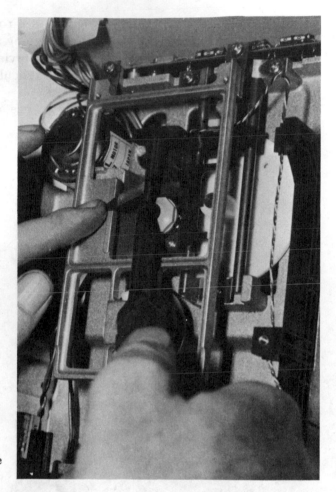

**FIG. 4–11** Changing the head load pad.

Some dealers will not charge their regular customers. When they do charge, the price is generally less than a dollar.

## REMOVING OR REPLACING THE DRIVE LED

The time may come when you want to remove or replace the drive LED. If the leads going to the LED are too short to allow you to remove the front panel of the drive, you may have to remove the LED. If it burns out (rare), you'll want to replace it as soon as possible. A burned-out LED will cause no problems, but it won't keep you informed of what is going on with the drive.

The LED is held in place with a small plastic retaining ring. Gently pry this off with a screwdriver as shown in Figure 4–12. You could break the ring or scratch the panel, so be careful. Once the retaining ring is loose, slide it out of the way. Press the LED toward the drive while prying apart the LED holder (a small metal clip) with a screwdriver. The LED should snap free from the front panel.

Replacement is nothing more than the reverse of this procedure.

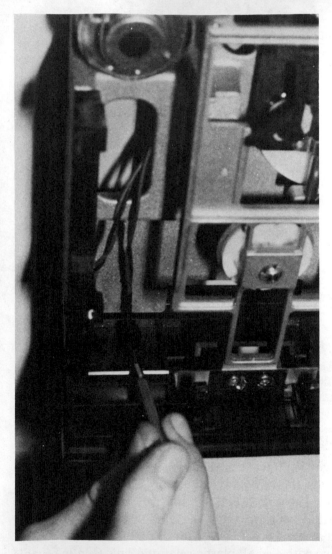

**FIG. 4–12** Replacing the drive LED.

*Williams: How to Repair & Maintain Your Apple Computer (Chilton)*

## DIAGNOSTIC STEPS

For all following steps, shut down the power and wait five seconds before flip-ping the switch on again. This resets the built-in protective circuitry and allows you to make accurate testings. It is also suggested that you perform each step at least twice, since the probes of your meter may not touch the right spots.

It is extremely important that you not create an accidental short by touch-ing the wrong pins and test points. *If your hands are shaky or you have any doubts, let a professional take care of the job.* You can do a lot of damage by being careless.

### STEP 1—TESTING THE LED

The normal response for a properly working drive is for the LED (the little red light) to come on just after the beep. If the light does not come on, there is an easy way to tell if the problem is in the LED or the power supply. (If it lights up, skip to step 2.)

Get out your meter and set it to read 1.5 volts DC. The common (ground) probe will touch test point TP2, TP3, or TP4 or any equivalent ground (such as the casing of the proper supply). The other probe should touch the right side of resistor R8, located at the extreme back center of the drive analog card (see Figure 4-13). Start the computer again and watch the reading you get. It should hit 1.5 volts just before the beep sounds and whenever the spindle is turning in the drive. If the reading is correct but the LED still does not light, the LED needs to be replaced. (See "Removing or Replacing the Drive LED.")

### STEP 2—TESTING FOR POWER

If everything is fine to this point, or if the first tests don't apply (the LED lights correctly), you will be checking for a voltage change across other points. Steps 2 and 3 are to determine if the circuitry used to activate the drive motor is work-ing. If the motor is obviously working correctly and if it operates when the LED lights up, skip to step 4.

Power comes into the drive on several pins of the drive cable (see Figure 4-14). Pin 1 is ground. The voltage between pin 19 and ground should be +12 volts DC. The voltage between pin 11 and ground should be + 5 volts DC.

Check for these voltages on both sides of the cable. First leave the cable plugged into the main cabinet. If the readings you get are correct, go to the next

**FIG. 4–13**  Location of resistor R8 and test points TP2, TP3, and TP4.

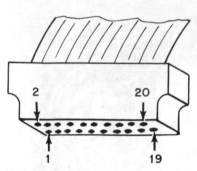

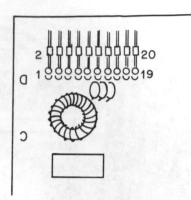

**FIG. 4–14** Pin locations on drive signal cable.  **FIG. 4–15** Pin locations on drive I/C

step. If they are not correct, check for the same voltages where the pins come out of the main cabinet (see Figure 4-15).

This is again that process of elimination. If power is leaving the power supply but not getting to the drives, you'll know that the problem is in the cable. If the pins coming from the power supply don't show the correct voltages, you can immediately suspect the power supply as the cause.

If these tests lead you to believe that the cable is at fault, set your meter to read ohms (resistance). The setting used doesn't matter. Touch one probe to a pin on one side of the cable and the other probe to the same pin on the opposite side of the cable. A reading of zero ohms means that the wire between those two pins is good. A reading of infinite ohms (full scale or no movement, depending on the meter you are using) means that the wire is broken somewhere along the cable. (This process—checking for continuity—is the best way to test any wire or cable that is not currently carrying a current. You can even use it to test the wiring between your stereo and speakers.) Usual repair is to replace the cable.

You can save a little time by checking only pins 1, 11, and 19, since these are the ones carrying power. But you are better off to take a few extra minutes to test the entire cable.

At the rear of the mechanical assembly is a small motor control board, also called a servo board. The voltage between the brown wire (at the top of this board) and ground should be +12 volts DC. Immediately beneath this wire is an orange wire. The voltage between this wire and ground should be about +5 volts DC. You can also check for the +5 volts at the front of resistor R1. Testing here is the same as testing at the orange wire. Figure 4-16 shows the

*Williams: How to Repair & Maintain Your Apple Computer (Chilton)*

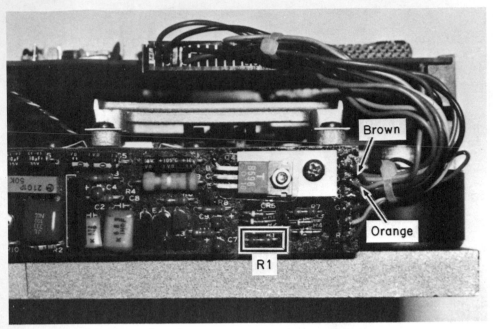

**FIG. 4–16**  Drive servo board.

brown and orange wires and R1. If the voltages are correct here but incorrect on the analog card (from step 1), the trouble is with the analog card.

When you have finished the above tests, you'll have a good idea of where the problem is. If power is leaving the power supply, the problem is with the drive or cable. A simple test eliminates the cable as the possible cause. Testing the brown and orange wires will tell you if the trouble is in the motor control (servo) board, the drive controller card, or the drive analog card or if you should test the power supply again.

Occasionally a problem with the power supply may not show up in testing. The Apple's power supply is capable of producing 60 watts. If too many devices are connected to it, the power supply simply can't keep up with the demands. If the readings you get are correct but your computer consistently fails when it is loaded, chances are the power supply is either being overloaded or is wearing out.

Try to operate the computer with fewer devices attached. For example, if you have two drives, disconnect drive 2 and try again. (Don't forget to shut off the power before disconnecting or connecting any device.)

*Williams: How to Repair & Maintain Your Apple Computer (Chilton)*

## STEP 3—TESTING THE MOTOR CONTROL CIRCUITRY

Set the meter to read 5 volts DC and connect the black lead (common) to TP4 or some other ground. With the power off and the drive connected, touch the red probe of the meter to pin 13 of the 74LS125 chip. (see Figure 4–17). Turn on the power. The LED should come on and stay on, and the reading on your meter should be 0 volts. If this doesn't happen, the chip or the drive interface board is bad.

**FIG. 4—17**  Location of pin 13 on the 74LS125 chip.

*Williams: How to Repair & Maintain Your Apple Computer (Chilton)*

Reset your computer. For the IIe, do this by pressing CONTROL-OPEN APPLE-RESET. For the II or II+, simply hit RESET or CONTROL-RESET. You should now get a reading of about +5 volts DC, with the drive motor and LED both off. Once again, if the results are other than this, the drive interface board is at fault.

For a two-drive system, load up drive 1 of the computer with any diskette that has DOS on it and that can be catalogued. The System Master or any initialized diskette should do. Try to get a catalog of a diskette in drive 2. The reading at pin 13 of the 74LS125 should be about 5 volts while the drive motor is off, should drop to 0 volts while the drive is looking for the directory (with the motor on), and should then go back to 5 volts when the motor shuts off again. If this doesn't happen, the drive interface board is faulty.

Set your meter to read 12 volts DC. The black probe (common) is still connected to TP4 or ground from the last step. The red probe touches pin 13 on the ULN2003 chip (see Figure 4–18). When the motor is off, you should get a reading of 0 volts. When the motor is going, the reading should be about 12 volts. If these readings are not correct, the drive analog card is bad.

## STEP 4—TESTING THE WRITE-PROTECT SWITCH

The notch on the side of the diskette activates (or deactivates) the write-protect switch inside the drive. When the notch is open, you can write data on the diskette and erase what is there. Cover this notch (e.g., with tape), and the data on the diskette cannot be changed. However, if this switch goes bad, the data and programs on the diskettes may be erased. If the drive malfunctions while the write-protect switch is faulty, you could find yourself with a blank diskette through no fault on your part other than inserting the diskette and applying power. If you find that this switch is faulty, DO NOT attempt to use the disk drive until you have made the repair.

If you suspect that the write-protect circuitry is faulty or if you want to make an occasional safety check, you can perform a very simple test. Take a diskette that has nothing of value on it. Cover the write-protect notch and try to write onto the diskette and then to erase it. If the switch is functioning properly, you won't be able to erase or change anything on the diskette.

At the back of this book (page 190) is a simple test routine that will check the write-protect switch. In this program, if the write-protect circuitry is functioning, you'll get a write-protect error. (The monitor should show WRITE ENABLED with the write-protect notch uncovered and WRITE DISABLED with the notch covered.)

Set the meter to read 5 volts DC. With the power off, connect the black lead to TP4 or ground and touch the red lead to the front of resistor R11 located on

**FIG. 4–18**  Location of pin 13 on the ULN2003 chip.

the right edge of the analog card (see Figure 4–19). Turn on the power. The reading should be 0 volts. If you get a reading, transistor Q2 (type 2N3906) located near the front right corner (see Figure 4–20) is bad.

Replacement of the transistor requires care. Too much heat will damage the inside of the new transistor and could even damage or destroy the board; too little heat will cause the soldered leads to give problems later (if not immediately). If you don't know how to solder correctly, leave the job to a professional.

You must also be careful to install the new transistor correctly. There are

*Williams: How to Repair & Maintain Your Apple Computer (Chilton)*

**FIG. 4–19**   Location of resistor R11.

*Williams: How to Repair & Maintain Your Apple Computer (Chilton)*

**FIG. 4–20** Location of transistor Q2.

three leads coming from the transistor. Viewed from the flat side of the transistor and from left to right, the leads are E (emitter), B (base), and C (collector). Refer to Figure 4–21 for pin locations. It's critical that the new transistor be installed *exactly* as the old one was.

After checking this transistor (or replacing it), check the write-protect circuitry. Set the meter to read 5 volts DC. The black lead goes to TP4 or ground. The red lead goes to pin 20 (back right pin) of the drive cable. With the power on, you should get a reading of 0 volts. Insert a diskette into the drive to activate the switch. The reading should jump to between 3 and 5 volts. If it does, the write-protect switch is okay.

The final test of the write-protect circuitry will tell you if the switch is at fault or if the drive analog card is bad.

Shut off the power and set the meter to read ohms (resistance). Locate resistor R8 on the drive analog card and the two solder points that are at the front left near this resistor (see Figure 4–22). Touch the probes to the two points. The reading should be near 0 ohms and should increase to near infinity when a diskette is inserted into the drive. If this happens, the switch is okay and the write-protect failure is due to a faulty drive analog card. If it doesn't happen, try the same test again, but this time push down on the write-protect switch with your finger. (The switch is located on the left side of the drive assembly about an inch inside the drive door.) If the test result is still bad, then the switch has to be replaced. If it failed when you inserted the diskette but passed when you opened the contacts of the switch, you may be able to adjust the switch.

## STEP 5—REPLACING AND ADJUSTING THE WRITE-PROTECT SWITCH

Replacing the switch is easy to do. Take off the drive cover and remove the drive analog card. The wires from the drive to the write-protect switch are soldered together. The switch is held in place by two screws. Take these out. Now you have enough room to use a soldering pencil on the leads. Installing the new switch is just the reverse procedure. Be careful not to overtighten the screws.

To adjust the switch, load in the switch testing program from the back of the book. Then remove the drive cover and turn the drive upside down. Insert

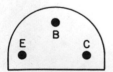 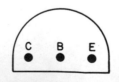 **FIG. 4–21** Typical transistor pin locations.

*Williams: How to Repair & Maintain Your Apple Computer (Chilton)*

**FIG. 4–22**  Location of resistor R8 and the two solder points.

a diskette (with the write-protect notch uncovered) part way. The diskette itself will now be keeping the contacts of the switch open. Loosen the two screws, rear screw first. As you loosen the front screw, the switch should rise slightly. As this happens the monitor should display the message WRITE ENABLED. Press down gently on the front setscrew until the monitor displays WRITE DISABLED. Tighten first the front screw and then the rear screw.

To test the adjustment, turn the drive on its side. Push the diskette all the way in. As the uncovered write-protect notch slides under the switch, the monitor should display WRITE ENABLED. As you pull the diskette out the screen should again show WRITE DISABLED. Do this check with a diskette that has the notch covered, with the covering tape pinched tight.

If you do not get the correct screen displays after a couple of attempts to adjust the switch, you probably won't be able to adjust it. Replace it with a new switch. If the write-protect problem is still there, chances are the drive analog board is bad and will have to be replaced.

## STEP 6—CHECKING THE PULLEY AND BELT

With the drive cabinet removed and the power off, turn the drive over. You'll see a pulley and belt (see Figure 4-23A). Turn the pulley by hand to check for sticking, binding, or uneven turning (Figure 4-23B). Look at the belt to make sure it is securely in place and to see if it is showing any signs of wear.

## STEP 7—CHECKING HEAD MOVEMENT

With the power off, remove the drive casing and drive analog card. This will allow you to see the read/write head (Figure 4-24). Gently move it with your finger (front to back). There should be a small amount of resistance to the motion, but the movement should be possible without any sticking or binding.

Partially attach the drive analog card again, leaving it just loose enough so that you can lift it to watch the heads. Reattach all connectors. Push the head to track 34 of the drive. Track 0 is the outermost ring; track 34 is closest to the center. Since the heads are in the back half of the drive assembly, track 0 is the closest to the door and the farthest from the rear of the drive. Track 34 is always closest to the spindle of the drive and to the center of the diskette. The head should be at track 34 as you begin this test. (You can also move the head to track 34 by turning the cam.)

Turn on the power. During loading, the head should move to track 0 and away from it again. (If the drive can't read the disk, the head will stay on track 0.) If the head does not go to track 0, the drive assembly may be bad and may have to be replaced. Perform the test a few times to be sure.

*Williams: How to Repair & Maintain Your Apple Computer (Chilton)*

**FIG. 4-23**   (A) Pulley and belt of the disk drive (B) Turn gently to check for sticking or binding.

## STEP 8—CHECKING THE DRIVE CABLE

In Step 2 you checked the drive cable (see Figure 4-25 for pin locations) to be sure that the wires that carry power to the drives were sound. You should have taken the few extra minutes to check the other wires in the cable for continuity at that time. (If you didn't, do so now.) The others carry various signals to and from the drive. A broken wire inside the cable can cause all sorts of trouble.

With the meter set for ohms (resistance), place one probe on one end of a wire and the second probe on the opposite end of the same wire. If the wire is intact, the meter will show 0 ohms. If the wire is broken, the meter will read infinite ohms.

## DRIVE SPEED ADJUSTMENT

There are several ways to test the speed of a drive. If you don't have the diagnostics diskette, you can test the drive speed manually by using a fluorescent light. The program in Appendix A can be used to keep the drive motor running. However, do not allow the drive to operate continuously for more than a few minutes at a time or you might damage the power supply.

*Williams: How to Repair & Maintain Your Apple Computer (Chilton)*

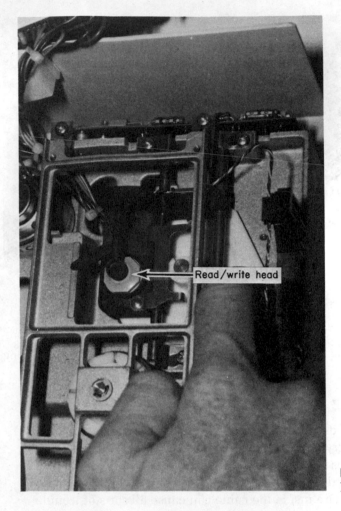

**FIG. 4–24**   Read/write
head.

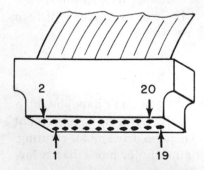

**FIG. 4–25**   Pin locations on drive signal cable.

*Williams: How to Repair & Maintain Your Apple Computer (Chilton)*

Remove the drive and tip it on its side. Insert a diskette to operate the motor, and watch the pulley under the fluorescent light. If the drive is operating at the correct speed, the marks on the outer ring should seem to stand still. (The inner marks are for 50-hertz power.)

If the speed is incorrect, adjustment is made by turning the variable resistor screw on the servo (motor control) board at the rear of the drive (see Figures 4–26 and 4–27). By watching the marks on the pulley (under the fluorescent light), you should be able to tell which way to turn the variable resistor for correct adjustment.

Easier and more accurate is to use the diagnostics diskette. Select the drive speed test (L). Remove the diagnostics diskette and insert an initialized scratch diskette (a diskette with nothing important on it, since the data will be destroyed), and press RETURN. The speed of your drive will be displayed to the nearest tenth of an rpm (for example, 299.7). If you are using a diagnostics diskette or another program that reads the rpm, the speed may vary a few tenths as

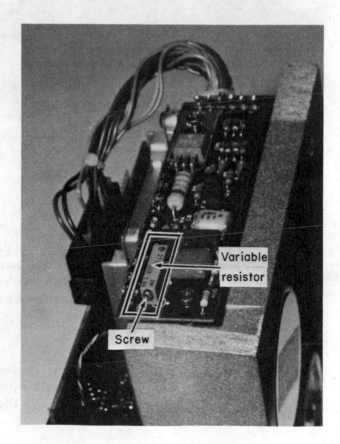

**FIG. 4–26** Variable resistor.

*Williams: How to Repair & Maintain Your Apple Computer (Chilton)*

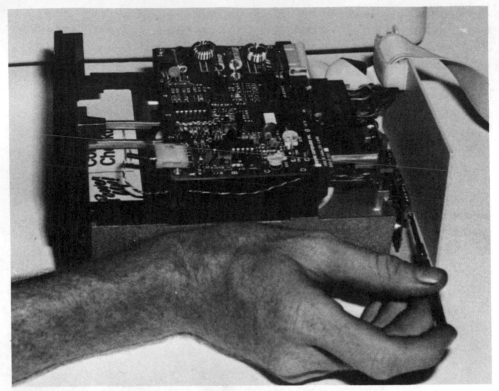

**FIG. 4–27**   Use a screwdriver to adjust the variable resistor screw.

the test runs. This is normal. Any reading between 299.0 and 301.0 is okay, with 300.0 being correct. (Some people prefer their drives to operate a little slower, claiming that the slower speed enables the drive to read the diskettes better.)

This test will automatically shut itself off after about three minutes. This is to prevent the power supply from being overworked. But three minutes should give you more than enough time to make the adjustment, which is again done by turning the variable resistor. If time runs out before you've finished the adjustment, give the power supply a while to cool before you start it again.

DISK DRIVE ANALYZER

Verbatim Corporation sells the Disk Drive Analyzer (shown in Figure 4–28) under its Data Encore subsidiary. The investment is small, considering what the program does. It tests for drive speed, head alignment, spindle clamping,

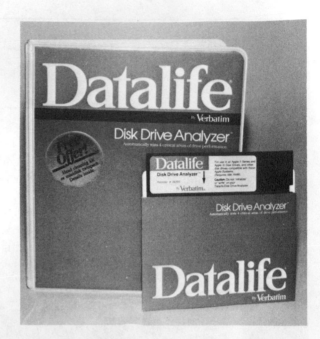

**FIG. 4–28** Verbatim Corporation Disk Drive Analyzer.

and read/write operation. After each test you will be told if the drive is good, fair, or poor.

Although you won't be able to make any adjustments with the program, it can keep you informed of the condition of your drives. A regular testing (which takes about two or three minutes) will alert you if the heads are going out of alignment or if something else is threatening your data. The drives are too critical a part of the computer system to be neglected until they fail.

## SOME OTHER PRECAUTIONS

You can avoid many drive problems simply by prevention. Keep the environment as clean as possible. Dust and other contaminants can create havoc with the drive.

Regular cleaning of the read/write heads is a good practice. How often you do this will depend on your surroundings and the degree of computer use. Don't skimp when you are buying a head cleaning kit. Get the best possible. (More information on regular cleaning and maintenance is contained in Chapter 7.)

If your drive has to be realigned or changed in any way, or if the drive speed has to be adjusted, you must make new copies of everything that has

STOP!

Don't do anything to your drive until you've made copies of all data recorded
on the maladjusted drive.

been recorded on the drive. If you don't, you could lose all the data that was
recorded on the maladjusted drive. Use that drive as the "source," with a drive
that you know is good for the "target."

The reason for this is that the faulty drive has recorded the data according
to the maladjusted-drive characteristics. If you try to read that data on a properly operating drive, you'll probably get nothing but garbage. By using the
faulty drive as the source, you're allowing it to read the data with the charac-

**FIG. 4–29**   Remove the four holding screws.

*Williams: How to Repair & Maintain Your Apple Computer (Chilton)*

teristics embedded. The good target drive will record the data the way it should be.

The Verbatim disk drive analyzer suggests running the test program regularly. With or without this program, you should test the drives occasionally. They are a critical part of the computer system. Realizing that the drive is going bad while it's recording some important data is too late.

## DISASSEMBLY OF THE DRIVE

Finding parts for the drive can be difficult. If your dealer won't sell them to you, you may have to be satisfied with reducing repair costs by being able to tell the technician what is wrong with the drive.

If you can get the parts, however, repair is generally simple. Disassembly can be done with nothing but a screwdriver. Move carefully to avoid damaging any parts. Refer to Figures 4-29 through 4-37, and take notes as you go.

## SUMMARY

The disk drives are probably the most critical part of your computer system. Unfortunately, they are also the devices most likely to cause troubles. This is because they are one of the few mechanical parts in the system. (The only other mechanical devices in the Apple are the optional cooling fan and the keyboard.)

If the drive malfunctions, existing programs may not operate. Data recorded on a misaligned or otherwise maladjusted drive can disappear once the drive is put back into shape again.

Only rarely will a drive suddenly fail. Most of the time it will give you warning symptoms, such as a faulty read or write. Both can be caused by other things, but both also indicate that it is time to check the drives.

Make drive checks and maintenance a part of your regular schedule. Clean the heads occasionally. Run diagnostics on them, with either the diagnostics diskette or one of the commercially available disk drive analyzer programs.

Preventive maintenance is the best possible means of ensuring that the drives will give you no problems. Backup copies of programs and data diskettes made while the drives are operating properly will help ensure that a drive malfunction is not a disaster.

*Williams: How to Repair & Maintain Your Apple Computer (Chilton)*

A

**Fig. 4–30** (A) Gently slide the cabinet off (B) The drive with the top cabinet removed.

B

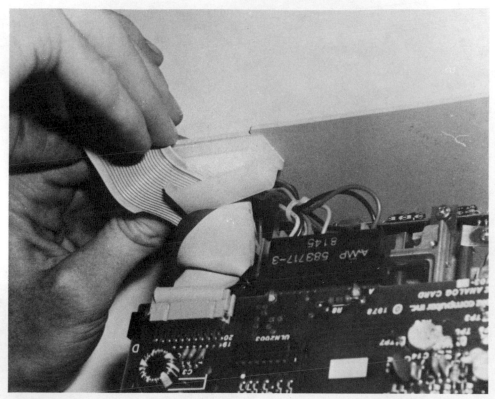

**FIG. 4–31** Remove signal cable from clamp.

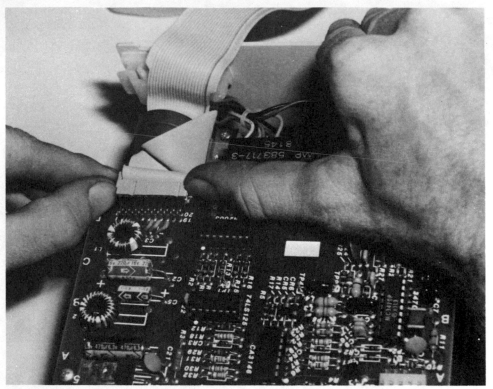

**FIG. 4-32**  Very carefully remove signal cable from the analog card.

**FIG. 4–33** Remove head control cable.

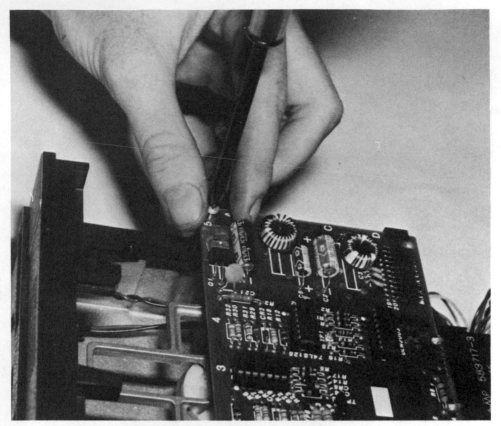

**FIG. 4–34**   Remove the analog card holding screws.

**FIG. 4–35**  Gently lift analog card free.

**FIG. 4–36** If you have to remove the bottom cabinet (and it is rarely necessary to do so), first remove the holding screws.

**FIG. 4–37** Lift the bottom cabinet off.

=================================

# Troubleshooting the Boards
## 5

Many things on the circuit boards cannot be tested without some very expensive equipment. Much of the time, the diagnostic steps you take will let you know which board is malfunctioning. Repair is usually by replacement. About the only time you'll be able to find the specific component that is causing the problem is when there is obvious damage.

However, you can easily test one critical circuit function: memory. This is the most common failure and also one of the more critical ones, since a failing memory chip can destroy hours of work.

## SYSTEM BOARD TYPES

The term *mother board* is used by Apple to describe the main circuit of the company's computers. The term has become so popular that it is often used to describe the system boards of other computers. Whether you call it a mother board or system board, it's the same thing.

The Apple II has two main versions of mother boards, depending on when the computer was built. Version 0 is the one used by earlier computers; version 1 (Figure 5-1) was introduced a few years later to correct some minor faults in the first board. The differences are described in the Apple II reference manual. (You can tell if you have a version 1 board by the presence of the single metal pin located on the upper right side of the board above the game I/O port and

*Williams: How to Repair & Maintain Your Apple Computer (Chilton)*

**FIG. 5–1** The mother board.

Williams: *How to Repair & Maintain Your Apple Computer* (Chilton)

below the four-pin auxiliary video output connector.) Few of these differences will matter to you. Both types work well.

The Apple II and II+ are configured to hold from 4K to 48K (version 1 of the mother board allows only 16K increments) of RAM on the mother board. You can increase this to 64K by adding a 16K language card, installed in slot 0. (The language card is only for the II and II+. The IIe is shipped with 64K already installed.) There are language cards available (not by Apple) that carry more than 16K extra, but few programs will use the extra memory after the first 16K.

The 6502 CPU cannot directly address (get at) more than 64K. The exception to this is the Apple extended 80-column board on the IIe, which allows 128K. See the reference manual that came with your computer for more information (e.g., on how the memory is mapped). For information on the IIc, see Chapter 10.

The mother boards of the IIe (see Figure 5-2) are all basically the same. There are no major revisions from the earlier IIe models. Most of these involve the way that the mother board is mounted to the chassis. The IIe has an advantage in that the mother board is designed to hold 64K of RAM. The overall design has also been simplified so that the IIe board requires fewer chips to do the same job.

## TESTING THE SYSTEM BOARD

Unfortunately, if something goes wrong with the system board, you won't be able to do much about it other than take it to an experienced technician who has the right test equipment.

First shut off the power. Check the system board carefully to be sure that all connectors are secure. Unplug them and reinsert, and then run the test again. Still with the power off, remove each of the cards, one at a time. Clean the silver or gold contacts (the "fingers" that go into the slots of the mother board) with a pencil eraser or other soft eraser. Do this away from the computer so that the eraser crumbs do not fall into the computer. Insert the boards again. Then gently press down on all ICs to make sure that they are in good contact with their sockets. Now try the system once again.

If things still don't function properly, get out your meter and set it to read 12 volts DC. You'll be testing the power flowing into the mother board by measuring across pins of the six-pin power supply connector located at the rear left corner of the mother board (see Figure 5-3). Push in the small tabs on the front and back of the connector that lock the cable into place, and pull the cable from the mother board to disconnect the power supply. Note that the connector com-

**FIG. 5–2** IIe mother board. *Courtesy of Apple Computer, Inc.*

**FIG. 5-3**  Location of mother board power connector.

ing from the power supply is a female end and that the pins are numbered (see Figure 5-4). Make a sketch to help you identify the pins on the mother board (a male connector) so that you will plug the two together correctly.

Touch the common probe (black) to either pin 1 or pin 2 of the cable coming from the power supply. Both are ground. Touch the red probe to pin 3 of

**TABLE 5-1**
**Value of Pins 1-6**

| Pin | Value |
|-----|-------|
| 1, 2 | Common (ground) |
| 3 | +5 volts ($\pm 3\%$) 2.5A |
| 4 | +11.8 volts ($\pm 6\%$) 1.5A |
| 5 | $-12$ volts ($\pm 10\%$) 250mA |
| 6 | $-5$ volts ($\pm 10\%$) 250mA |

*Williams: How to Repair & Maintain Your Apple Computer (Chilton)*

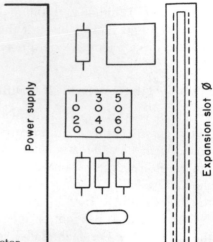

**FIG. 5–4**  Pin locations on power supply connector.

the cable and turn on the power. If you get a reading of 4.85 to 5.15 volts, the power supply is working in the 5-volt range. The power supply could be bad if the reading you get is outside this range (see Chapter 6).

If you get an acceptable reading, check the voltage across the 12-volt side. With the black probe still touching either pin 1 or pin 2, touch the red probe to pin 4. The reading you get should be between 11.1 volts and 12.5 volts. If the readings for both the 5-volt and 12-volt outputs are correct, the power supply is providing the correct voltages. This means that the system board is at fault. If the readings don't match, the power supply is probably at fault. Go to "The Power Supply" in Chapter 6 and run that series of tests.

If all readings are correct but the computer will still not power up, there are three possibilities. The power supply may be wearing out and be incapable of producing the needed amount of current. One of the other boards (including the mother board) may be faulty and pulling too much current for the power supply to keep up. Or you may simply be overloading the power supply yourself.

In the case of a worn power supply, about all you can do is get a new power supply. Fortunately, this is rarely necessary. The next two tests will help determine this. But before you yank out the old power supply, go to Chapter 6 and continue testing with the information under "The Power Supply."

To test the other boards for drawing too much current, follow the procedure from Chapter 2 on removing the boards one at a time (with the power off each time you remove a board) to find the one at fault. If the power supply will still not run the computer with all peripheral boards removed, you'll know that the problem is either with the mother board or with the power supply. Go to Chapter 6 and thoroughly test the power supply. If it passes all these tests, chances are the mother board needs to be replaced.

## USING THE DIAGNOSTICS DISKETTE

This book is available as a part of a package that includes a diagnostics diskette. The program and its operation are described in detail in Chapter 11. The diagnostics diskette will test several critical parts of the mother board. Test B checks out the ROM chips on board (see Figure 5-5 for location). Test C will show if the CPU is faulty. (See also "Memory" in this chapter for details on how to test the installed RAM.)

The Apple II has four or five ROM chips. The II+ has six ROM chips, and the IIe has two. For each model, load up the diagnostics diskette and select B. Press RETURN to begin testing and ESCAPE to stop. The diagnostics disk will cause these chips to generate a checksum, which is then compared with a value stored in the test program. If the two values are the same, the ROM chip being tested is good. If the values are different, the screen will show you which chip has failed.

The upper-left part of the display (see Figure 5-6) will show you how many errors have been counted. The upper right signifies the number of times the ROM chips have been tested, with each pass being a completed test of all ROM chips. Beneath will be the listing of the ROM chips (C0 and E0 for the IIe; D0, E0, F0, D8, E8, F8 for the II+). Next to each label will appear either GOOD or BAD, to let you know if a particular ROM chip is malfunctioning. Beneath the dashed line, the screen will remain blank unless the test finds a checksum error. If an error is found, this area will show which ROM chip is faulty. (For example, if ROM chip E0 showed an error, you'll see displayed: E0 CHECKSUM ERROR.)

The ROM testing will continue until you press ESCAPE. Usually you will want to let the testing continue through a number of passes. If the problem is intermittent, you may want to let the testing continue through 50 or more passes.

Option C on the diagnostics diskette is a test for the 6502 CPU (see Figures 5-7 and 5-8 for location). This chip is the heart of your computer. It tells the computer what to do, when, and how. The test is similar to the one for testing the ROM chips. Once you have selected option C, begin testing by pressing RETURN. The testing is stopped by pressing ESCAPE. The left side of the screen (see Figure 5-9) will display the number of errors found. The right side shows how many completed passes have been made. Beneath this will appear CPU

**FIG. 5–5** Location of ROM chips on mother board.

*Williams: How to Repair & Maintain Your Apple Computer (Chilton)*

```
        SYSTEM ROMS TEST                         SYSTEM ROMS TEST
        --------------                           ------------
        PRESS ESC TO EXIT                        PRESS ESC TO EXIT

  00000 ERRORS        PASS 00032            00000 ERRORS        PASS 00045

  D0 ROM GOOD         D8 ROM GOOD           C0 ROM GOOD         E0 ROM GOOD
  E0 ROM GOOD         E8 ROM GOOD           ----------------------------------
  F0 ROM GOOD         F8 ROM GOOD
  -----------------------------
```

**II and II+**                                          **IIe**

**FIG. 5–6**   ROM test screen.

STATUS — > and either GOOD or BAD. Beneath the dashed line will be any error messages.

On the diagnostics diskette is a test for peripheral cards (test F). This test will check not only the cards but also the slots of the mother board. Instructions on how to perform this test are found in Chapter 11.

## ELIMINATING THE OBVIOUS

Before you go to a lot of trouble or expense, make sure that you've eliminated all other possible causes of trouble. Open the cabinet and inspect the inside. Is there anything that could be causing an accidental short (like a screw that has fallen onto the board)? Are all option and adapter cards plugged firmly into place? Are all cables and connectors secure? (Unplug and reinsert; clean the contacts with a pencil eraser, *always with the power off* before removing or plugging in a card.)

Outside the cabinet, are the plugs and cables secure? Even more important, are they in the right places? Things can be plugged in backwards if you are careless. Cables, such as the keyboard cable, have a small arrowhead indicating which pin is pin 1. If you're not paying attention, you might plug the connector in incorrectly (rotated 180 degrees) and mess something up. Outside it's all too easy to have something plugged in incorrectly (into the wrong port, for example).

You should know the purpose of each expansion card. For example, a circuit card that is meant to allow you asynchronous communications (as through

**FIG. 5–7**   Location of CPU on the II and II+.

*Williams: How to Repair & Maintain Your Apple Computer (Chilton)*

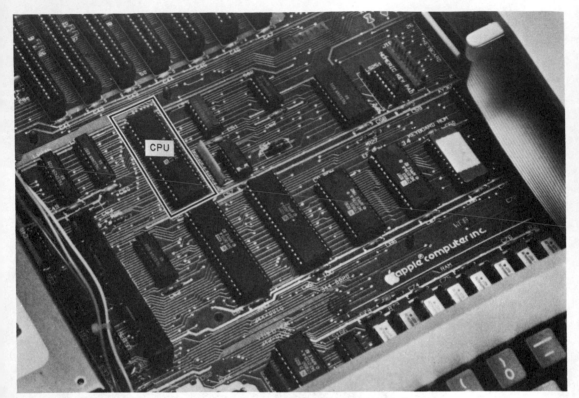

**FIG. 5–8**  Location of CPU on the IIe. *Courtesy of Apple Computer, Inc.*

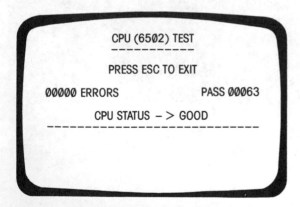

**FIG. 5–9**  CPU test screen.

*Williams: How to Repair & Maintain Your Apple Computer (Chilton)*

a modem) has a serial port. Since you know that the port is serial, you won't have to worry about recognizing it as being female or male (except when it comes time to connect it to the external device). Usually you don't have to worry about the number of pins on a cable, or their orientation.

If everything seems fine, disconnect all external devices and try again. If the error disappears, it was caused by one of these devices. Plug them in one at a time (with the power shut down each time). If the error does not disappear, remove all internal options and go through the same procedure.

## REMOVING THE MOTHER BOARD

If tests indicate that the entire mother board has to be replaced (this is rare), you may wish to do the work yourself. To remove the mother board, take off the case and disconnect everything going to the mother board. Be sure to make detailed sketches so you'll know exactly how everything goes back together. Remove the screws that hold the mother board in place (Figure 5-10A). Then, with a needlenose pliers, squeeze the top of each of the plastic snap connectors on the mother board and pull up on the mother board slightly so that the connectors do not snap back into place (Figure 5-10B). Gently lift the mother board out. If it doesn't come easily, you've missed a screw or snap connector. DO NOT use force!

## SETTING THE SWITCHES

Some cards have switch settings. You will see them mainly on printer and communications cards, clock cards, and some others, such as the Z-80 card. The switches will select such things as baud rate and line feeds. If the switches are set improperly, the device and the computer will seem to be malfunctioning.

The manual that comes with the particular device is your best, and often only, guide as to how to set the switches. The simple solution is to read that manual. Close attention to detail is important.

## TESTING MEMORY

RAM allows you to throw data into the memory and to retrieve it in any order. Without this your computer would be able to do very little. RAM is measured in bytes, more often in kilobytes. Generally, the more RAM you have, the more you can do.

The address bus of the 6502 CPU allows for direct access of 64K in memory

*Williams: How to Repair & Maintain Your Apple Computer (Chilton)*

A

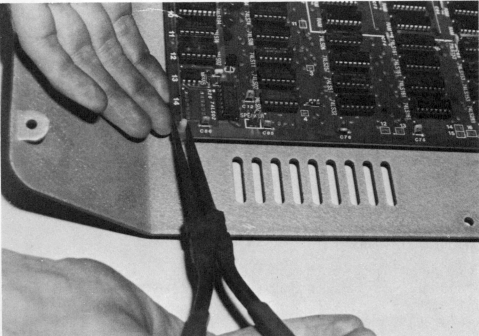

B

**FIG. 5-10**   Removing the mother board.

(ROM and/or RAM). In the Apple, the range from $C000 to $CFFF is set aside for peripheral cards and certain I/O functions. ROM normally starts at $D000 and continues to $FFFF. Soft switches inside the Apple allow RAM or ROM to be mapped over the ROM on the mother board. Thus, the 16K on the language card is mapped from $D000 to $FFFF, with another 4K mapping into $D000 to $DFFF. Sounds confusing but it works. It can be even more complicated when you start getting more RAM on the card, and more soft switches.

A soft switch is a software switch, not a physical switch. It is toggled by being accessed with a read or a write from the software. In the Apple, this switch can be given a single address or a range of addresses. By accessing this range, the soft switch is toggled from one side to the other.

On the IIe, some soft switches can be read to determine which side they are on. In other words, soft switches are used to determine which of several devices are to be selected. An example is the RAM and ROM of the computer. A soft switch allows either one or the other to be active.

Basically, the CPU looks for whatever it gets. The RAM is set to end at 48K. From here the Apple uses bank switching to allow programs to access more than 48K of RAM. Bank switching means that more than one bank of memory is usable in a single addressing range and that a soft switch determines which of the active bank switches is set. A more detailed description is in the reference manual that came with your computer. (The IIe reference manual is a separate purchase.)

The memory board is set in rows, called *banks*. One bank equals 64K of RAM on the IIe, either 4K or 16K on the II, and 16K on the II+. Eight chips make up each bank. Each chip represents a particular data bit. The data bits are numbered from 0 to 7, with bit 0 located on the left side of the mother board. As mentioned, the IIe uses high-capacity RAM chips and has all 64K in one bank. The II and II+ have banks arranged with either 4K or 16K per bank, with the front row usually used first. Knowing the location of each bank and bit is necessary if you're going to track down a failing memory module.

If you have additional RAM installed (such as with the 16K language card), the RAM chips on the option board may not be labeled. This makes finding the malfunctioning RAM module more difficult. The easiest way to do it is to swap the chip on the expansion card with the chips on one of the banks on the mother board. Better yet, and much safer, is to have an extra set of RAM chips on hand, or at least one or two extra chips known to be good. The diagnostics program and a bit of deductive reasoning will now point out exactly which chip has failed.

In doing this, you must be careful that the chips on the expansion card are compatible with those on the mother board. For example, if the mother board is using 16K chips and the expansion card is using 64K chips, you cannot swap them. You can tell if you have a 64K chip by looking at the number on the top of the chip. If it reads xx64 (4164 is the most common), the chip is 64K and should not be plugged into the mother board unless you have a IIe. The 16K chips are labeled xx16 (4116 is the most common).

## USING THE DIAGNOSTICS DISKETTE

Test A on the diagnostics diskette checks the main memory of the computer for malfunctions. As with other tests, RETURN starts things and ESCAPE stops them. The number of errors found is displayed on the upper left, with the number of passes shown in the upper right. Beneath this are the words MEMORY CHIP STATUS — > followed by spots for each module location (as seen from looking down from the top of the computer). The II and II+ have three layers of eight (see Figure 5–11); the IIe has a single line of eight spots (see Figure 5–12). When a G appears, the module at that location is good. If the module is bad, an asterisk (*) will appear, along with an error message beneath the dashed line.

There are two basic error messages: BANK SELECT ERROR and DATA ERROR AT LOCATION XXXX. The first indicates that the program was unable to test a certain part of the memory. Often this means that the problem isn't with the RAM chips but with the mother board. A data error message will give you the data location of the error as a decimal address. Replace this chip and run the test again.

Some RAM problems will not be found right away. Running the test just a few times may not result in location of the problem chip. If you suspect that the computer malfunction is due to a RAM chip, let the test run for several hours. This allows the routine to check each chip many times to find a hidden malfunction.

Option P on the diagnostics diskette allows you to print the results of the tests. If you wish to run the RAM test over a long period of time but don't care to sit there with it and jot down notes, set up your printer and select P. It will ask you to confirm that you want to send the results to the printer (with Y or N as your choices). It will then display ENTER PRINTER SLOT #. This is usually slot 1, but the program will support the printout if your printer adapter board is in another slot. Once you've entered this, the program will return you to the main menu and allow you to select whichever tests you wish to run.

This option (sending the results to the printer) will continue until you once again select P and enter an N when it asks, PRINT TEST RESULTS?

*Williams: How to Repair & Maintain Your Apple Computer (Chilton)*

**FIG. 5–11** Location of RAM chips on the II and II+.

*Williams: How to Repair & Maintain Your Apple Computer (Chilton)*

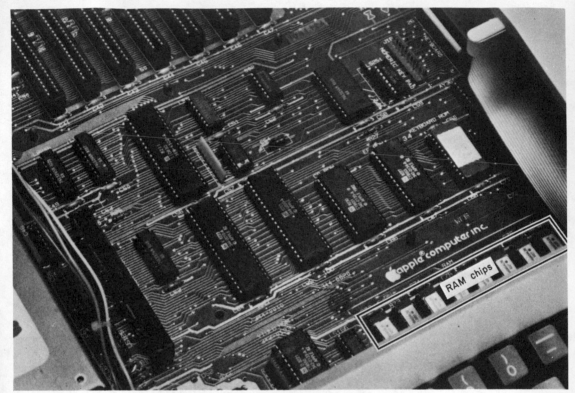

**FIG. 5–12** Location of RAM chips on the IIe. *Courtesy of Apple Computer, Inc.*

CHECKING THE MODULES

When you've located the failing module, you can test it by swapping it with another. The easiest way to do this is to switch it with another module in the same bank. When you run the test again, the error code should show that the faulty chip has changed position.

For example, if diagnostics indicates that module 5 has failed, swap it with module 1 in the same bank. The new error code should now show that there is a malfunction with module 1 and that module 5 is good. If it doesn't, try another swap within that bank. (For example, swap the suspected module now in socket 1 with the same module in bank 2. The error code should now be in bank 2.)

If this doesn't change things, the bank might have a more severe failure. Try a swap with another bank that seems to test okay.

With a IIe, since you have only one bank of RAM, you'll have to swap the chips with a set from somewhere else. A dealer can't be expected to lend you a set, but perhaps you have a friend who will.

If you don't have the diagnostics diskette to spot the failing module, you have little choice but to swap each of the RAM chips in turn with one that you know is good. This is a time-consuming chore and won't help much if more than one chip has gone bad. Faster, but more expensive, is swapping the chips a bank at a time. However, the cost of a full bank of RAM chips for testing purposes is more expensive than buying the diagnostics diskette.

For swapping chips, invest in an IC extractor, as mentioned in Chapter 1. This tool will help prevent accidental damage to the chips. Handle the ICs gently. Touch them as little as possible and avoid touching the pins at all.

## TESTING OTHER BOARDS

Without sophisticated test equipment, you probably won't be able to find the specific problem with a circuit board. However, you can perform a few simple tests on your own.

First visually check the suspected board. Is it snugly connected? Are all cables going to it attached tightly? Have any of the components worked loose? (Don't forget to shut down the power before removing or inserting any board, cable, or device and before pushing on the components to make sure that they are seated properly.)

Try cleaning the contacts with a high-quality electronic cleaner. Don't use a television tuner cleaner or anything that could leave a residue. If you don't have a cleaner around, you can use a soft pencil eraser (as shown in Figure 5-13), making sure that you don't get any particles inside the computer.

If the suspected board is new to your system, consider the "Has it ever worked?" question. Have you made any other changes to the system?

If you have the diagnostics diskette, use it to test the suspected board. The diskette will test most peripheral cards. Details on how to set up and run the various tests are found in Chapter 11.

Make a note of the error code and what is happening or not happening. This should help you isolate the problem to a single board.

Unplug the suspected board and run the diagnostics again. If the error code disappears (the routine should show an empty slot), you'll know that the board is at fault. If the error is still there, the problem is elsewhere in the system. You can also disconnect all external devices attached to the board. If the error disappears when the card is in place but the devices are disconnected, the problem might be in an external device.

*Williams: How to Repair & Maintain Your Apple Computer (Chilton)*

**FIG. 5–13**   Cleaning the contacts.

## SUMMARY

Diagnosis of board malfunctions begins by determining which component is acting up. If a drive is doing strange things, don't waste time testing the RAM board. If the printer is acting up, don't waste time fiddling with the driver adapter.

By observation and note taking, you should be able to isolate the malfunctioning board quickly.

As always, take some time to visually inspect for the obvious. Are all cables and wires firmly attached? Are they connected correctly? Is the board compatible with the Apple? Has it changed something else?

Most of the time repair is done by replacement. This is because tracking the failure to a single component usually requires a lot of time and some special equipment.

RAM boards and the memory modules on them can be tested quickly and easily. The diagnostics diskette will do most of the job for you by finding the module or modules at fault. From there it is simply a matter of swapping the faulty modules with good ones.

Fortunately, if a board operates when you first install it, it will probably continue to function for many years. No maintenance is required other than to change the battery for the built-in clock.

*Williams: How to Repair & Maintain Your Apple Computer (Chilton)*

# Power Supplies, Keyboards, Printers, and Monitors

# 6

You can connect a number of different options and devices to your Apple. Because there are so many different options and manufacturers, it is impossible to cover them all. We have included only the most common options in this chapter. These should give you some basic guidelines for repair.

The diagnostics diskette will help isolate problems in many of the options available. Use this and the information in Chapter 2 before you begin poking around in the machinery. The steps taken in Chapter 2 are what should have brought you to this chapter. (You just might find that the problem is in a place you didn't suspect at first.)

As mentioned in Chapter 2, some options manufactured by companies not "approved" by Apple may give false readings during diagnostics. Keep this in mind while trying to find the problem. For example, diagnostics might indicate that there is a problem with the internal modem, when in fact there is no problem at all in that device.

## THE POWER SUPPLY

The driving force behind the Apple (and all things electronic) is the power supply (see Figure 6-1. It does just what the name implies. It takes the 120 volts at 60 cycles per second from the wall outlet and changes it to a clean, steady 5- or 12-volt-DC supply. Table 6-1 lists power supply specifications.

*Williams: How to Repair & Maintain Your Apple Computer* (Chilton)

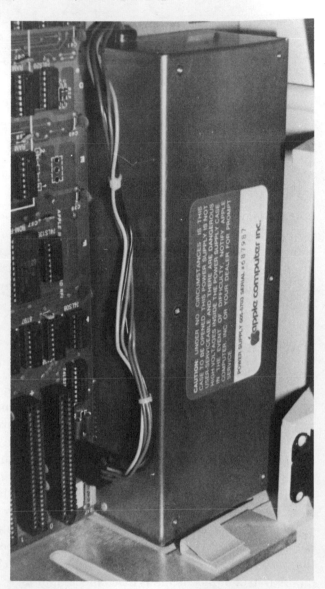

**FIG. 6–1** The power supply.

Normally it does its job just fine and gives no problems. Unlike the power supplies of some other computers, the power supply of the Apple is relatively tough. Chances are there won't be a problem with anything relating to the supply other than the mechanical on/off switch in the back.

If the power supply is acting up, you may not be readily able to spot it as

*Williams: How to Repair & Maintain Your Apple Computer (Chilton)*

### TABLE 6-1
#### Power Supply Specifications

| | |
|---|---|
| Input Power | 107–132V AC (120 nominal) @60Hz; 2.5A |
| DC Output | +5V ± 3% 2.5A |
| | −5.2V ± 10% 250mA |
| | +11.8V ± 6% 1.5A continuous, 2.5A intermittent |
| Maximum Case | 130°F (55°C) |
| Temperature | −12V ± 10% 250mA |

the problem. If the computer seems completely dead, the power supply may be responsible, but so may the system board or a combination of other things. If your computer seems to be operating normally except for a data read/write problem, you may be inclined to blame the memory board or the drives, while the real cause may be the power supply. Don't replace it until you know for sure.

## POWER SUPPLY DIAGNOSTICS

If nothing happens when you flip the power switch, you are likely to accuse the power supply without further thinking. This symptom could mean that the power supply has died. It could also mean that something else is wrong.

Remember that the fan (if you have one) is wired directly to the incoming 120-volt line. If the fan isn't working, chances are the problem is outside the computer. (It would be rare for both the fan and the power supply to give out at the same time.) If the fan is operating, power is getting to the computer.

If the problem is outside the power supply, the power supply will try to reset itself every half second until the problem is eliminated. Each time this cycle occurs, the oscillator passes through an audible range and produces a soft click. If you hear a steady "click, click, click," the power supply is working, and the cause of the problem is that (1) a supply voltage is short circuited to ground, (2) the power supply cable is disconnected, or (3) a supply voltage is outside its normal range.

To find out if the power supply is faulty, take the following steps.

### STEP 1—CHECK INCOMING POWER
If power is obviously present (i.e., the power light on the keyboard lights up or you hear the clicking), you can skip this first check and go to steps 2 and 3. If nothing is happening, begin with this step.

*Williams: How to Repair & Maintain Your Apple Computer (Chilton)*

The first things to check are the power cord, the plug, the outlets, and the power switches. Once you have done this and know that power is getting *to* the power supply, you have eliminated the obvious and started the process of isolating the problem.

As mentioned in Chapter 2, you can use a lamp or any number of other things to check the outlet for power. However, you are better off checking it with a meter (see Figure 6–2). The power supply operates in the ranges of 107 volts and 132 volts. A lamp will operate beyond these ranges without any apparent difference, but the power supply of the Apple will automatically shut itself down (affecting everything except the fan). Until you've checked the outlet with a meter you won't know for certain if the problem is in the computer or in the lines that supply the outlet. (More information on using a meter to check outlets is given in Chapters 1 and 2.)

If power is getting to the power supply but nothing is happening, move on to step 4 or 6.

### STEP 2—RUN THE IIE SELF-TEST
The IIe is capable of performing a quick and simple self-test. Run it if you can.

**FIG. 6–2** Checking an outlet with a meter.

*Williams: How to Repair & Maintain Your Apple Computer (Chilton)*

It may give you information that will assist you in locating the problem. Consult the list of error codes in Appendix B for an explanation of the codes.

### STEP 3—USE THE DIAGNOSTICS DISKETTE

The diagnostics diskette (described in Chapter 11) does not have a test specifically for the power supply. However, the diskette can be used to help eliminate other devices as being the cause of the trouble.

### STEP 4—CHECK EXTERNAL DEVICES

Because of its built-in protective circuitry, the power supply in the Apple will shut down if something else in the computer is faulty and is drawing too much current. This protects both the power supply and the devices. It can also lead you to believe that the power supply is dead when in fact it is doing just what it was designed to do.

If the problem is in one of the connected devices, such as a printer or drive, you can find out easily. Shut down all power and disconnect everything that is

**FIG. 6—3**  Disconnecting internal devices.

*Williams: How to Repair & Maintain Your Apple Computer (Chilton)*

connected to the computer. Apply power again. If there is still no power, go to step 7. If you have power flowing again, you know that one of the devices is at fault. To find out which one it is, merely plug them in one at a time (with the power shut down each time) until the power fails again.

Shutting down the power before connecting or disconnecting anything is extremely important. If you don't shut down the power you could destroy the computer.

### STEP 5—CHECK INTERNAL DEVICES

If disconnecting external devices doesn't help, the next step is to apply the same idea to internal options (see Figure 6-3). With the power off, disconnect all internal options, including the drives and the option boards. If power now flows, you know that one of these is causing the trouble. Shut off the power and reconnect these devices and options one at a time until the trouble is found. Again, remember to shut off the power *each time* before making a new connection. You don't want to destroy your computer for the sake of the second it takes to shut down.

**FIG. 6—4**   Location of power supply connector.

*Williams: How to Repair & Maintain Your Apple Computer (Chilton)*

It's possible to get inconsistent results if the power supply is just starting to go. It may not be able to produce sufficient current. The easiest way to find out is to go through steps 4 and 5 a couple of times, inserting the devices in different slots and in a different order. (Make sure you don't insert a board into slot 0.)

If a device is suspect, go to the appropriate section in this book for further help (e.g., if the offending device is the memory board, go to Chapter 5).

If nothing changes after removing all internal devices and options from the power, go to step 6.

### STEP 6—CHECK VOLTAGES TO THE SYSTEM BOARD

This step involves the use of your multimeter set at 12 volts DC. The test points are where the cable from the power supply plugs into the system board (see Figures 6-4, 6-5, and 6-6). Pin locations are marked on the cable. Disconnect the mother board. Even though the mother board is disconnected, the power is

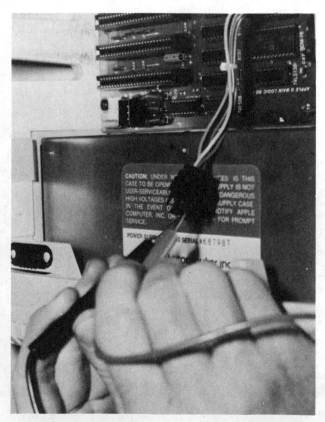

**FIG. 6-5** Checking power supply output.

*Williams: How to Repair & Maintain Your Apple Computer (Chilton)*

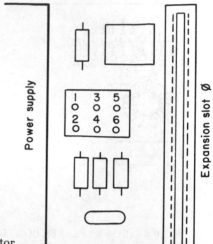

**FIG. 6–6**   Pin locations on power supply connector.

on during these tests. You must be extremely careful not to cause any short circuits.

First you'll be checking the voltage between pin 1 and pins 3 and 4 (pin 1 is common). You should get a reading of 4.8 to 5.2 volts between pins 1 and 3, and 11.1 to 12.5 volts between pins 1 and 4. If you don't get these readings, move immediately to step 9.

If these voltages aren't correct, you'll know that the problem is definitely in the power supply. All you can do is replace the faulty unit (with an exact match). If the voltages are correct, proceed to the next step.

### STEP 7—CHECK DISK DRIVE POWER

This step tests if power is getting to the drives. It can be skipped if the drives seem to be operating correctly. If the drives have been causing trouble, you can find out quickly whether the problem is in the drives, the power supply, or the drive cable.

In Chapter 4 you learned that there are two basic types of drives: Alps (with an "Apple Computer, Inc." label) and Shugart (with a "Shugart Associates" label). Testing for power is similar for both, and the pins are in the same location (see Figure 6–7).

Power to the drives comes from the power supply. The pins are labeled, so there shouldn't be any problem identifying which are which. The common lead of your multimeter goes to any one of the ground pins (1, 3, 5, or 7). Check each of the power-carrying pins (13, 15, 17, and 19 for 12 volts; 11 and 12 for 5 volts).

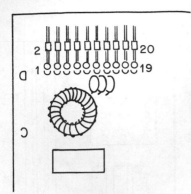

**FIG. 6–7** Pin locations on drive I/O.

### STEP 8—CHECK SPEAKER CONTINUITY

The speaker is connected to the mother board with a two-prong plug. Disconnect the plug from the mother board. Set the meter to read resistance (ohms) in the ×1 range. The reading across the speaker should be approximately 8 ohms. Some meters will not measure this accurately. However, this isn't important; you are merely checking for continuity (see Figure 6–8). A speaker with a relatively low resistance is fine. An infinite resistance means that the speaker is "open" and needs to be replaced.

Unfortunately, if the computer has passed all tests to this point and the speaker tests okay as well, the problem is in the mother board, which often means that a more expensive repair is called for. For further diagnosis go to Chapter 5.

### STEP 9—CHECK RESISTANCE ON THE MOTHER BOARD

If your computer has passed all previous tests, you have one more thing to check, the resistance of the mother board. As with all other things connected to the power supply, if the mother board tries to draw too much power (e.g., with a short), it will cause the power supply to shut itself down. Some of the previous steps will have indicated this. Step 9 will verify if the problem is in the mother board or the power supply.

With the power off and all devices removed, disconnect the power connector from the mother board (see Figure 6–9). This will allow you to probe the main circuits of the system board with your meter. Set your meter to the ×1 range. There should be a low resistance between 5 volts (pin 3) and ground (pin 1) and between 12 volts (pin 4) and ground (pin 1). (There will probably be some resistance because the signal from the multimeter will go through ICs.) If there

**FIG. 6–8**   Checking speaker continuity.

is a very high resistance, then something is wrong with the mother board or ICs on the mother board.

## THE KEYBOARD

Each key is a switch. The keys are similar to the buttons on a joystick but much more durable. As you press down on the key, contact is made and the appropriate signal is sent to the computer by the circuitry.

Some of the IC chips on the keyboard are extremely sensitive to static electricity. They can be damaged if you touch them with your fingers. If you must touch them, be sure that you are well grounded, perhaps by placing your other hand on the case of the power supply or by touching some other reliable ground.

Apples have gone through many different keyboard designs. The early Apple IIs, for example, had two completely different types of keyboard. One had all the keys and electronic circuitry on a single board, while the other had

*Williams: How to Repair & Maintain Your Apple Computer (Chilton)*

**FIG. 6—9**  Location of mother board power supply connector.

a small, separate board (the encoder board) that held some of the keyboard circuitry.

The two most common keyboard problems are failure to detect a keystroke, and keyboard bounce. More often than not, the cause of the trouble will be the keyswitch itself. Although the keys are durable, after a million presses they can quit working.

There are three different keyswitches used by Apple; screw-on, snap-on, and nonreplaceable. The first two types can be tested and replaced (see following sections). The third, and newest type, can be repaired only by replacing the entire keyboard and cannot be tested.

Testing the keyswitch is easy. To do this, shut off the power and remove the computer's case. Set your meter to read resistance (ohms). On the bottom of the keyboard you'll see that each key has two traces (parts of the circuit board that act as wires). Touch the probes to each of the traces. The reading should be infinite, showing that there is no pathway. When you press the key, the resistance should drop almost to zero. If this doesn't happen, the keyswitch needs to be replaced.

Inside the keyboard are the electronics, which handle the signal from the keys to the computer. Unlike the keys themselves, the electronics are prone to damage from fluid. To protect your keyboard, keep all fluids away from it.

You've probably heard some horror stories about liquid falling into a computer keyboard. One of the strangest I've ever heard involves a man who decided that his two-month-old baby sitting on the keyboard in front of the computer would make a cute photo. The child had an "accident." Obviously so did the keyboard. The acidic fluid caused bad connections on the soldered components and even damaged the circuit board. This made a simple repair impossible. The keyboard had to be replaced.

## CHANGING A SCREW-IN KEYSWITCH

To change this type of keyswitch, you will need a high-quality soldering tool and some experience in using it. If the heated tip touches the circuit board for more than about three seconds, the heat could lift the tracing from the board. Melt the solder on the pins of the switch. A desoldering tool is helpful in removing the melted solder.

Next, remove the screw that holds the switch in place. Turn the keyboard over and pull on the cap of the key. If you've done everything right, the key should come out easily. Don't force it.

Reverse this process to install the new switch. Once again, be careful when using the soldering tool. If you don't have experience with soldering, leave the job to a professional. (Soldering is not as easy as it seems.)

## CHANGING A SNAP-ON KEYSWITCH

Following the same cautions as above, melt the solder from around the pins and remove it with a desoldering tool. Turn the keyboard over and remove the key cap. Inside you'll find two clips that hold the keyswitch together. Pinch these clips with a needlenose pliers. The key assembly should come apart easily.

Installation of the new key is the reverse of this. Be careful not to force anything.

*Williams: How to Repair & Maintain Your Apple Computer (Chilton)*

## TESTING THE CABLE

Before you give up and toss away the keyboard, check the continuity of the keyboard cable. It's unlikely that one of the wires inside is giving trouble, but it is possible. To check for continuity, remove the cable from both the keyboard and the computer and then set your meter to read ohms (×1). Touch the probes to the ends of each wire (e.g., pin 1 to pin 1; see Figure 6–10).

## THE PRINTER

Many different printers are available. Each has its own characteristics and construction. One may require a partial disassembly just to reset the switches. Another may have a built-in memory buffer. Still another may have the dual capabilities of both computer printer and standard typewriter. There are differences in speed, print quality, and printing technologies. The printer may require a serial connection or a parallel connection, or it may allow you to choose which you prefer. Some may even require special software patched to your regular programs. With the wide range available, it isn't possible to give repair information on all makes and models.

The manual that came with your printer is the best source for specific information. Become familiar with it and find out what capabilities your printer has and how to take care of various problems that could come up.

Many printers give you the option of connecting them either as a parallel device or as a serial device. Parallel is the more common means of connecting a printer for several reasons. If the computer has one port of each type, the serial port is usually kept open for communications. Devices such as modems require a serial connection. Connecting the printer as a parallel device keeps the serial port available.

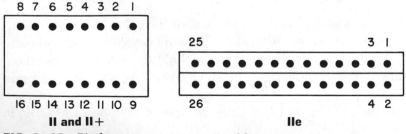

**FIG. 6–10** Pin locations on keyboard cable.

*Williams: How to Repair & Maintain Your Apple Computer (Chilton)*

## PROBLEMS WITH PRINTERS

Because the printer is a mechanical device, it is prone to more wear and tear than most things connected to the computer. It has at least two motors (for head and platen) and may have more. The print head moves back and forth across the platen and either spins (as with a daisy wheel printer) or has a print head that makes characters by punching at the paper with wires (dot matrix printer). All this motion causes wear. It can also create fair amounts of heat. If allowed to build up, heat can cause all sorts of damage, both mechanical and electronic.

The first thing to do is to get out the manual for your printer and familiarize yourself with the information. Many manuals give specific error signals to let you know what has gone wrong. Also included will be information specific to your printer, such as how to remove the platen and other parts in case of a paper jam and how to load the ribbon.

Paper can jam as it feeds through the printer. Even single sheets can cause a jam. Printers that use multiple sheets (with sheet loader or tractor) are even more prone to jams. Jams tend to be more common if your printer is connected as a serial device. When a jam occurs, the printer can grind to a halt. Sometimes the jam isn't apparent. A few printers require a fairly complicated disassembly to correct the jam.

If the ribbon isn't installed properly, strange things can happen. Part of a character might be printed, with the other part weak or nonexistent. The printer might stop working entirely or print a couple of characters and then act as though the signal had stopped.

In some printers, a small switch senses the end of the ribbon. As the ribbon reaches its end, the switch stops the printer. This switch can also signal that the ribbon is used up if the cartridge isn't attached properly or if the switch fails. Other printers feed the ribbon through continuously. When the print gets light, you replace the ribbon.

Many printers have a safety switch in the lid. If you lift the lid, the switch tells the printer to stop. It will tell the printer the same thing if the lid isn't closed all the way or if the switch is faulty.

If the printer is not making an impression, remove the paper and look for indentations. The print head will make indentations in the paper if it is working, even if the ribbon is not. If the paper has the marks from the print head, the ribbon or ribbon-advance mechanism is causing the problem.

Many adjustments are possible with most printers. There are the usual spacing and forms thickness (number of sheets) adjustments, the release catches, plus others. Just as a typewriter won't function properly if the adjustments aren't correct, neither will the computer's printer.

*Williams: How to Repair & Maintain Your Apple Computer (Chilton)*

Checking for all of these things goes back to the standard rule, "Look for the obvious." The majority of the time the problem will be something very simple.

By performing occasional maintenance checks and cleaning the printer, you can greatly reduce the malfunctions. Clean the ribbon guides, the print shield, and the inside of the machine. A buildup of ink or paper dust can cause problems. If your printer has a built-in self-test, run it occasionally. (Run it once when you first get the machine and are sure that the printer is operating correctly. How else will you know what the results of the test are supposed to be?)

This self-test allows you to carry the diagnostics one step further. If the test shows that the printer is operating correctly, you'll know that the problem is in the printer interface, the cable, or the computer. You can eliminate the cable by testing for continuity with your meter. The diagnostics diskette can tell you if the printer adapter card and port are functioning correctly. About the only thing left is the interface in the printer itself.

## PRINTER DIAGNOSTICS

If there seems to be no power going to the printer, check the outlet, the power cord, and the fuse before assuming that the problem lies in the power supply. If power is obviously present, you can skip all power checks and go to the more detailed diagnostic steps, such as running the printer's self-test (if it has one).

If power is getting to the printer but nothing happens, check once again all cables, connectors, switches, and the software itself. You can eliminate some things simply by knowing that the printer once functioned as it should.

The self-test cycle of the printer (if it has one) should give you a good idea of where the problem is. If the self-test operates, the printer is probably fine. The problem is then most likely with the card inside the computer or with the cable. You can easily eliminate the cable as the possible cause by using your meter.

Disconnect the printer cable. With the meter set to read resistance, touch the black probe to a pin on one end of the cable, and the red probe to the same pin on the opposite end. A reading of near 0 ohms means that the wire between the pins is good. An infinite reading shows that the wire in the cable is broken or that those pins are not used.

The cable between the computer and the printer has up to 25 pins. Some are not connected to anything and will give a reading as if the wire inside were broken. The printer manual should tell you which pins are used and which are not. Without this, you'll have to take the cable heads apart to know the wiring.

*Williams: How to Repair & Maintain Your Apple Computer (Chilton)*

Inside, the wires are probably color coded. If even one wire is broken inside the cable or isn't making proper contact with the connector, the printer might refuse to function.

Refer to the manual for the correct switch settings. If the switches aren't set correctly, the printer will punch out meaningless characters. It is also important to have the software you are using installed (made compatible with your printer). The procedure for this is usually explained in the software documenation.

The diagnostics diskette (see Chapter 11) will help you spot the problem, within limits. The printer test will send a print pattern to the printer. Because the pattern differs slightly with different printers, run the test while you know that your printer and printer controller are functioning properly. Then keep the hard copy of the test handy for comparison.

Locating the problem is again a process of elimination, with the diagnostics diskette providing a means of testing the printer once you think you have the problem fixed.

Change just one thing at a time, in a step-by-step process. It's sometimes tempting to use a shotgun approach, but this can only add confusion.

## THE MONITOR

Monitor problems are usually obvious. The screen may be blank. It may show an incorrect display. It may have an image that is tilted, too small, too large, out of focus, too dim, and so on. If the image on the screen is out of whack, the problem is probably with the monitor. If the problem isn't in the monitor, there are only a few other places it could be. You can find out quickly by running a few simple tests.

Certain monitor tests, symptoms, and characteristics of regular television sets differ from those of color monitors. Others are identical for both systems. As always, begin with the simplest things first.

A client brought in a malfunctioning computer system. "The monitor isn't working," he said, "and I just bought it a few days ago." You should be asking yourself the paramount question, "Has it ever worked?"

"I tried everything I could think of. I know that my old monitor was working."

"Have you tried reconnecting the old monitor?"

The client did this and found that everything was working as usual again. After a few more questions, it was discovered that the new monitor had been moved from place to place quite often and that more than one control knob had been changed.

*Williams: How to Repair & Maintain Your Apple Computer (Chilton)*

## MONITOR DIAGNOSTICS

It's easy to touch, bump, or otherwise change the various control knobs on the monitor. An example is the horizontal hold. If this knob is out of adjustment, the display may show nothing but a nonsensical pattern. The contrast and brightness controls as well as the color and tint knobs are also easily knocked out of adjustment.

Check all the knobs, including the on/off button, before you do anything else. You may have to turn them quite a bit to get any results. The proper adjustment may require changes in more than one control. It is a good idea to maladjust a properly working monitor—only after you've carefully recorded the correct control settings. This will teach you how to work the controls and will show you what kinds of things can appear on the screen if the controls are improperly set.

A sudden change in the display during operation indicates that something besides the manual adjustments is wrong. A simple adjustment probably won't help. Shifts during operation usually indicate a problem in the monitor itself.

Check all cables and connections. (You should know by this point if the adapter card will support the kind of monitor you are using. If the monitor has ever worked properly, you'll know that the adapter card is the correct one.) If the connections seem solid, disconnect the cables and run the diagnostics again. If the error is the same, you'll know that the problem is with the adapter card. If the error disappears, then the problem is either with the cables or the monitor.

You can test the cables for continuity by using your meter set to read ohms in the ×1 range. Place one lead on a pin on one side of the cable, with the other lead touching the same pin on the opposite side (see Figure 6–11). The reading should show almost zero ohms. If it shows a large resistance (usually a reading near infinity), a wire inside the cable has broken and you'll have to replace that cable. Go from pin to pin until each wire in the cable has been tested.

Once you have eliminated the monitor and cable as the cause, you'll have located the problem: the mother board.

Before you go to the trouble and expense of replacing the card, check to see if it has been installed correctly and if there is any obvious damage, such as burned or loose components.

Is the card pushed all the way into the expansion slot? Try removing and reinserting the card to make sure the contacts are solid. If you have a cleaner that will not leave a residue, clean the contacts on the board as shown in Figure 6–12. (All lubricant-type cleaners leave a residue, so be sure to avoid them.) If

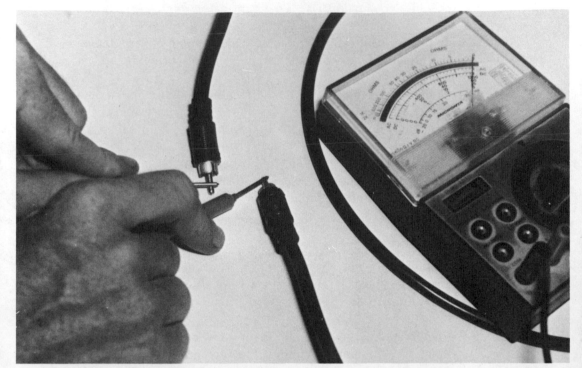

**FIG. 6–11**   Testing monitor cable for continuity.

**FIG. 6–12**   Cleaning the contacts of a board.

you don't have a cleaner, you can use the eraser of a pencil to clean the contacts. Be careful to brush away all the rubber tailings before bringing the board near the computer again.

A final check involves using another monitor, cable, and perhaps computer (one at a time in a process of elimination). If you don't have a friend with an Apple, try a dealer. Many dealers will be more than happy to help if they know that you'll be purchasing the replacement part(s) from them.

If the problem still persists, the fault is probably in the mother board. Repair is by replacement in almost all cases. Don't forget that the old mother board will probably have a trade-in value.

## SUMMARY

Power supply problems are not always obvious. The built-in protective circuitry will shut down the power if something is wrong elsewhere in the system. A nothing-happens situation does not necessarily mean that the power supply is at fault.

Testing the power supply involves eliminating devices one at a time and taking a few voltage measurements. Within just a few minutes you should be able to isolate the problem to something specific.

The keyboard is tested continually. You test it yourself merely by using it. If pushing a key consistently does nothing, or if the key simply feels wrong, you'll know that it's time to perform more thorough testing or to replace the individual key or the keyboard itself.

Printers are famous for giving troubles. They are mechanical devices with at least two motors spinning along. Just connecting the printer in the first place can be frustrating. Once it is working, you can keep it that way by some occasional maintenance, such as cleaning out the paper dust.

As with printers, a malfunction of the monitor is generally obvious. It also requires that you pay careful attention to what is happening and what is not happening. The computer will test the monitor, but only to a certain extent. It can't tell if the monitor is displaying correctly. This is up to you. Learning what to expect from the monitor ahead of time will help you. Altering the adjustments while the monitor is working properly can guide you later on if a problem comes up.

*Williams: How to Repair & Maintain Your Apple Computer (Chilton)*

# Preventing Problems: Periodic Maintenance
## 7

The Apple is so well designed and constructed that there isn't much to be done as far as maintenance goes. As with all computers, most of the activity takes place inside the circuits. There is very little to adjust or clean, almost nothing to go wrong.

Even so, you can reduce repair costs and aggravation by performing a few simple maintenance checks now and then.

## THE ENVIRONMENT

The most important factor in the overall health of your computer system is its surroundings. The more dust and other contaminants, the more often your system will give you trouble.

One owner used her computer to keep track of her electroplating company. The computer was kept separate from the plant, but not separate enough. The acidic fumes were obvious, both to the nose and to the computer. Every few months she would have a major computer failure. Twice in the first year she had to replace the drives, once the entire system board.

Another company hired an operator who smoked heavily. Within a few months one of the drives was malfunctioning. When opened, it was discovered to have a heavy layer of grime. The second drive was in nearly as poor condition.

*Williams: How to Repair & Maintain Your Apple Computer (Chilton)*

The more pure and clean the computer room, the better. You won't be able to eliminate all contaminants, but this isn't really necessary. Your goal is to reduce the number of contaminants.

When dusting around the computer, use a damp (*not* wet or dry) cloth. This will pick up and trap the dust instead of spreading it around or tossing it into the air. Don't use anything like a feather duster anywhere around the computer. After cleaning the surrounding area, clean the computer equipment. Dust will gather on the equipment, particularly on the monitor screen.

On the cloth, use a gentle cleaner or just plain water (squeeze out the cloth so that it is barely damp). Be especially careful with the monitor screen. Some have a nonglare coating that can be damaged. Do not have open containers near the computer, it's too easy for liquids to spill. When they do, they have the unfortunate tendency to fall exactly where they can do the most damage (Murphy's Law at work).

Be very careful about getting liquids of any kind into the electronics of the computer. A slightly damp cloth can be used to clean the cabinet, monitor, printer case, and outer edges of the keyboard. DO NOT use a damp cloth inside anything electronic. You're asking for trouble if you do. Dust will have very little effect on most electronic components.

The inside can be cleaned with a vacuum cleaner (with a soft brush) if dust has built up. Move the vacuum slowly to avoid circulating the dust. Vacuuming isn't really necessary, however, because the components inside the computer aren't sensitive to dust as long as it is dry. The internal parts of the printer, in contrast, are more sensitive to dust. Paper gives off a surprising amount of dust, which can collect in all the wrong places and jam the mechanical parts.

The computer circulates air (and dust) inside it for cooling. Dust may enter the disk drives, the spot where it can do the most damage. Although a little dust is unlikely to affect the circuits, it's murder on anything mechanical.

## DRIVE HEAD CLEANING

There are two opinions about head cleaning. One is that it is never necessary and can only cause damage. The other is that it is necessary after every so many hours of use and that it will cause no damage at all.

Each is partially true. Obviously, you're better off leaving the heads alone as much as possible. But when cleaning is necessary, it should be done. You can't afford to wait until the recorded data is full of errors because of a dirty head.

Anything abrasive used on the heads is obviously capable of damaging them. The same goes for other parts in the drive. If you stay with a well-known brand of cleaning fluid, you should have no trouble.

The idea of cleaning the heads after so many hours can also be misleading. The key is your own environment. If you work in a sterile environment and use only the best-quality diskettes, deposits will be minimal. You won't need to clean the heads very often. In contrast, if you're a heavy smoker or keep the computer in a poor-air environment (shame on you!), you will have to clean the heads more often.

Head cleaners can only take off recent deposits. If you let deposits build up over a long period of time, they become permanent parts of the heads. No cleaning kit in the world will take off such deposits, at least not without destroying the head at the same time.

There are various ways of cleaning the heads. Before people realized how much damage could be caused, they used abrasive cleaners. These literally scratched away the contaminants—and the surface of the head. Fortunately, very few of these cleaners are around now.

The next step is a nonabrasive head cleaner and a bottle of fluid. Generally such a package is less expensive and also tends to last longer. Again you have to be careful that the rotating pad isn't too abrasive. (Stick with a reputable brand and you should be safe.)

Be careful not to oversoak or undersoak the pad. Both can cause problems. If the pad is undersoaked, the abrasive action is increased and the head won't be cleaned as well. If it is oversoaked, the excess fluid will slosh around inside the delicate parts of the drive. It will evaporate before too long, but in the meantime it can cause problems. Worse yet, there's no way to know if harmful materials have been deposited in the drive or if other damage that will show up at a critical moment has been caused.

The most expensive head cleaners are presoaked. Figure 7-1 shows a kit that contains a presoaked cleaning pad. Carefully measured amounts of cleaner are already on the diskette cleaning pad, which means that there is virtually no risk of the cleaning fluid (and the stuff dissolved in it) dripping into places where you don't want it.

The disadvantage of such a cleaning kit is that the cleaning diskette not only costs more to begin with but also wears out sooner. Since there is never an excess of cleaning fluid, the fluid will evaporate more quickly from the cleaning pad, making the diskette useless, if not dangerous. This won't happen if you follow the directions, though. The advantage is that you have much less risk of damaging the heads, the drive itself, or other diskettes you put in. The

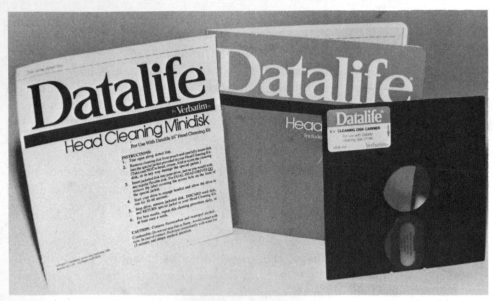

**FIG. 7-1**　Head cleaning kit.

lower risk easily warrants the higher cost; the difference in price just isn't all that much.

You can clean the heads manually, of course. This involves some work on your part and a certain degree of risk. You'll have to remove the drive case and the circuit board inside. You simply can't access the heads safely otherwise. Each time you do this, you take up valuable time and risk damage to the circuit board. There is also the danger of knocking the heads out of alignment. Generally this is not the way to go about it.

If you choose this method, you'll need some clean cotton swabs (the tighter the better) and cleaning fluid. Isopropyl alcohol will do, but only if it is pure. Much of the alcohol available to the general public has water and certain oils in it. Some has other contaminants that could be harmful. Using alcohol that is available off the shelf is often a great way to guarantee damage to the heads and drive. Technical-grade alcohol is available through chemical supply companies. Be sure that you specify *pure* isopropyl alcohol with *no* contaminants.

You can also use fluid head cleaner for audio tape players. Again, it is important that you get the best possible. Don't try to save a few pennies. The heads of your disk drives are too important and too expensive to replace.

*Williams: How to Repair & Maintain Your Apple Computer (Chilton)*

## DISKETTES AND SOFTWARE

The more you use a diskette, the more the chance of trouble. In Chapter 3 you learned how tough, and how delicate, a diskette is. The best-made diskette can still present problems.

The major problem is the allocation table or catalog. Each time you use the diskette, the computer seeks out this track to learn what you have on the diskette. This means that the life of the diskette is directly proportional to the number of times you use this track.

The second major problem is editing. Changes in a diskette file can scatter the file all over the diskette. A disjointed file is much more prone to hand out errors than one that is in a logical sequence.

Think of the file as several very long letters to friends that you write over a period of a year or more. Before you send them, you want everything to be just right. So you go back to the loose pages and add little notes. After a while, you have a massive stack of scribbles and pages. It would be almost impossible for you to keep track of which pages go to which friends.

The computer doesn't have quite this much trouble, but it still has to keep track of which changes you've made to which files. Those changes may end up scattered all over the diskette, and it could be like having a heavy wind get hold of your letter files.

The solution is to make copies often. You have two choices. The COPYA routine will make an exact duplicate of the original. This method is fast and will copy everything on the original, including the blank temporary files used by some programs and your scattered edited files.

The FID or FILEM routine is slower and will ignore those temporary files. This program has the advantage of arranging a disjointed original on the copy diskette in the correct order. Fragmented files are thus restructured.

Instructions for using COPYA, FID, and FILEM are in your manuals. If you don't already know how to use these commands easily, learn!

Programs used often should be copied regularly if the program allows this. Many don't in order to thwart software pirates. The new copy also has a new allocation track, which will bring a worn program back to life again.

Don't wait until the program or data diskette has failed before making the backup. Do so immediately! If you have diskettes that are used often and that haven't been backed up recently, put down this book and do it—NOW! If the backup sits on the shelf or in the box for a year, great. You don't make the backup to use; you make it to ensure that a diskette failure doesn't knock you down and out. (Wouldn't it be great if you had a backup heart? Backup software is nearly as important.)

Before filing away the backup copy for safekeeping, take a moment to test it. If it is a program, try it out. Don't just see if it will load—actually work it. If it is a data diskette, check it to see if the data has been transferred intact and without errors.

## DIAGNOSTICS

If you haven't already done so, read through Chapters 2 and 11 on how to operate the diagnostics diskette. (Instructions come with the diagnostics diskette if you buy it separately.) Even if you don't have a diagnostics diskette at this time, become familiar with what it can and cannot do.

Assuming that your computer system is functioning properly, run the diagnostics program right away. Become familiar with how things are supposed to look. If something goes wrong later on, you'll know better how to track it down. It's a good idea to run the diagnostics diskette regularly—how often will depend on your use of the computer. (Once a month will probably be fine. I use my computer heavily, and the once-a-month routine serves me well.) If you wait too long, you could easily forget how things are supposed to look. Even notes you've made (you have been making notes, haven't you?) may not make much sense a year from now.

If you have a IIe, run the built-in self-test occasionally. The few minutes spent in letting the computer test itself thoroughly is a worthwhile investment.

The Verbatim Disk Drive Analyzer program mentioned in Chapter 4 is an excellent and a relatively inexpensive means of keeping a close eye on the most critical part of your system, the drives. Run this program regularly and you'll spot most common problems in the drives before they do serious and irreversible damage.

## OTHER STEPS

It's all too easy to get used to the computer's power and forget that the machine is quite delicate in certain ways. Each hour you spend with flawless operation tends to make you forget that things can go wrong.

Make it a habit each time you sit down to the computer to review in your mind all the things that can go wrong. Pay close attention to what it is doing and how things are working. The more you use a particular program or function, the more important this attention is.

If you have a friend with an Apple, sit down and use your friend's machine occasionally with your programs and data diskettes. Then give your friend a session with your computer. This will tell both of you quite a bit about how well the computer system is functioning.

For example, if a diskette or program functions perfectly on your machine and not the other, something is wrong with one of the two. Don't assume that the problem is with your friend's Apple. Even if your own computer seems to be operating correctly, it could be having problems. For example, if the heads in your drive are misaligned, you'll be recording information that can only be read on a drive with heads that are misaligned in exactly the same way.

Regular swapping of computer time will help keep you informed of any serious malfunctions. It gives you a basis for comparison that many people don't have. If you don't have a friend with an Apple, contact your dealer. Chances are the dealer will let you use one of the floor machines for a short time, especially if you've been a good customer.

Lacking this, consider joining a user group. Other members in the group are likely to be after the same sort of cross-checking. As you check your system, they are checking theirs. (You'll also end up with a valuable source of information, and plenty of new friends who share your interests.)


## SUMMARY

There is very little maintenance to be done for your computer system. Invest a few minutes per week and you've done just about everything necessary to keep your system running smoothly.

The environment around the system is critical. The cleaner you keep the general area, the fewer problems you'll have and the less maintenance you'll need. Keep dust and other contaminants away from the computer as much as possible.

If you ignore the drive heads for too long, they could develop a permanent buildup of particles that no cleaner can remove. The result will be faulty reading and writing of data at unpredictable times. A periodic cleaning of the heads, with the best-quality head cleaning kit, will help keep the heads working for many years. How often you clean the heads will be determined by how much your computer is used and what the surroundings are like.

The most delicate part of a computer system is the software. Handle the diskettes carefully. Just as important, make backups of all diskettes regularly. The cost of diskettes is low compared with the cost of replacing lost programs or data.

Every so often, run the diagnostics diskette. It's unlikely that you will find any problems, but this step will help spot malfunctions before they become serious. It will also help remind you of how the diagnostics *should* perform.

*Williams: How to Repair & Maintain Your Apple Computer (Chilton)*

**TABLE 7-1**
**Maintenance Routine**

---

**Daily**
1. Make backup copies of all data diskettes you've been using. This should be done at the end of each session and periodically during the session.

**Weekly**
1. Give the computer area a quick clean to cut down the amount of dust.
2. Perform a FID or FILEM routine on any data diskettes that have been used heavily.
3. Run Disk Drive Analyzer, if you have one.
4. Clean disk drive heads, if necessary.

**Monthly**
1. Thoroughly clean entire area, including the inside of the printer.
2. Clean disk drive heads.
3. Test devices and equipment that are rarely used.

**Occasionally**
1. Test backups already made.
2. Make new backups of important programs and data, if necessary.
3. Run diagnostics—even if nothing has malfunctioned.
4. Spend some time with your diskettes on someone else's Apple.

---

Table 7-1 is a guide for maintenance routine performance. The frequency of the routines will be determined by your usage of the system. For example, if you work at the computer for only a few hours per week, you probably won't need to clean the drive heads weekly. This listing is only a general guide. Set up a schedule for your own circumstances.

*Williams: How to Repair & Maintain Your Apple Computer (Chilton)*

# Adding to Your System
## 8

Just when you think you have everything for your computer, something else comes along. The printer you have may not be printing fast enough for your needs, or perhaps the character quality needs to be improved. If you bought the computer with just one drive, you're almost guaranteed to want a second drive very soon. That black and white display or adapted household television set might be replaced by a high-quality computer monitor. You're certain to be adding new software programs from time to time.

Even if you don't add something to your system, the day may easily come when an existing piece of equipment requires replacement. The steps in replacing a device are nearly the same as those in adding the device for the first time.

This chapter will show you how to handle some of the most common additions. Your circumstances will be slightly different in some cases, depending on the equipment you're using. However, the general guidelines presented here should help.

A good rule is to change only one piece of equipment at a time. For example, if at all possible, don't add a new printer and a new, untested printer cable.

It's important that you become as familiar as possible with the new device as soon as possible. If it comes with an installation manual (most accessories do), read it cover to cover—don't skim or skip. Certainly don't try to install the equipment while reading the manual for the first time.

The biggest problem that most people run into is being in too much of a hurry. That new memory board you've been saving up for arrives and seems to cry out for immediate use. Off comes the cabinet and in goes the board with little more than a cursory glance at the installation manual. The result—the thing doesn't work.

Slow down. And then go slower yet. If you don't understand the instructions, go back and read them again. Have a very good idea of what you're doing before you start and you're much more likely to have the installation work. You'll actually save time—and much frustration—by taking the time to become familiar with the necessary information first.

The Apple reference manual that came with your computer is a helpful guide for many installations. In it are lots of tips and instructions. Even those sections that don't seem to apply to what you're doing can end up helping. It doesn't matter if the accessories you have were manufactured by a company other than Apple. Much of the information in the reference manual applies to all additions you'll make.

Before actually installing anything, go through the procedure at least once mentally. Do you know which steps to take when?

Check and double-check any switch settings you've had to make, both in the computer and in the new device. If no switches are to be changed, be sure that you know this as well.

Finally, NEVER install a device while there is power flowing. Shut off the switch. There is rarely a need to unplug the computer. In fact, keeping it plugged in provides a safety by grounding everything. When you leave the computer plugged in, be aware that the line and power switch are still hot.

## DRIVES

If you've been trying to operate your computer with just one drive (or none at all), you'll know how severely limited you are. Not many people will be satisfied with just one drive for very long. Fortunately, the Apple is designed to make installation of drives (and other devices) easy.

Shut down the computer and pop off the cover by pulling up on the two back corners. If you have plates covering the back slots, remove the one that the first drive cable goes to. Slide the 20-pin connector through the plate. Make sure that the drive cables can reach the connector on the drive controller card before you fasten the plates to the computer again. Fasten the plates and plug in the drive cables.

Be sure to distinguish correctly between drive 1 and drive 2. Drive 1 connects to the upper 20-pin connector and drive 2 connects to the lower one. Be very careful in plugging in the cables. If the connector is attached improperly,

*Williams: How to Repair & Maintain Your Apple Computer (Chilton)*

damage to the disk drive and controller card will result. As soon as you apply power, the 74LS125 chip on the drive analog card will explode.

Although standard procedure, these instructions are only a general guide for your reference. Check the instructions that come with the new drive and with the controller card. If you're using a drive other than the Apple Disk II, you may have to make a few minor adjustments to the drive. It's also possible that the controller card will not support the drive, depending on which card and which drive you have.

Most users place one drive on top of the other, with drive 1 being the upper unit. How you do it is up to you. It will make no difference in the actual operation of the drives. DO NOT put other devices on top of the drives. Some users place the monitor on the drive cases. Doing so invites troubles, in both the mechanical and the read/write functions of the drives (see Chapter 4).

The Apple drive controller card is capable of handling up to two disk drives. Usually you use only one or two drives. If you require more floppy drives, you may install another drive controller card, which will allow you to use two more disk drives.

## HARD DRIVES

There are many "Winchester" drives on the market for the Apple II series. The more popular ones are the 5M- and 10M-byte models that work with Apple II ProDOS, DOS 3.3, Pascal, and CP/M and with Apple III's operating system.

A hard drive usually comes with its own power supply built in. The drive should also come with an adapter or interface board that is installed in the Apple to control the drive, as well as all cables and software needed to support the drive under whichever DOS the computer may be using. Software should be included to back up the data in the hard drive and to handle any other file management operations the user might need.

As with almost everything else, a number of manufacturers make hard drives, each of which is different and requires different commands. Some are only marginally compatible with the Apple. Do your research carefully and make sure the drive comes with everything you need before you let price guide you.

For example, most drives have a backup utility (a means of storing the disk files on floppies for data safety). Some support the use of special cassettes as backup. The commands required might be completely different from those in the DOS manual, so be sure to find out how to back up your programs and data from the dealer. (The same is also true with the FORMAT and INIT routines.)

There are two basic methods of backing up data and programs from a hard drive. One is simply to use a copy program, such as FID (FILEM on the IIe) and place the programs and data on floppies for safety. This can be tedious. You will have to copy each file individually, because most copy programs will stop once the floppy is filled. Copying this way requires the use of many diskettes. You simply can't copy the contents of a 10M-byte hard drive onto a single .14M-byte floppy. An additional disadvantage is that many copy programs will not be able to access data on the hard drive, which is why the hard drive you buy should come with the software needed to back up the data.

If you're going to back up your hard drive with floppies, number each of the diskettes and label them carefully. This way, if you ever do need to restore a crashed hard drive, you'll know exactly what was in there and in what order.

The second method of backup is to use a special cassette. This method offers the advantage of placing the entire contents of the drive on a single cassette instead of on a number of diskettes. It has two major disadvantages.

The first is the additional cost of purchasing and connecting the backup machine. This isn't much of an expense when you consider the value of the data and programs stored on the hard drive, but it is one more cost.

Second and more important, there is no way to check the integrity of the backup copy on some systems unless you erase everything on the hard drive and try to reload from the backup cassette. (This may also be true of backing up your programs and data files on floppies.) Trouble is, by the time you find out that the backup is no good, the original is gone.

A customer bought a new hard drive, the cassette backup, and all the things that go with them. He dutifully backed up everything in triplicate, including a massive 2.5M-byte data file for his business. One day the hard drive crashed and refused to boot. All the data on it disappeared into electronic limbo.

No problem, he thought. He got the hard drive repaired and went to restore the data from the backups. Then he found out that the backup program had malfunctioned and that the backup tapes were blank. It was a software, not a mechanical, problem and was easy to fix—but that did nothing at all to restore the lost data. (Generally the tape backup is considered one of the most efficient and safest methods.)

You can reduce the risk by using only the highest-quality diskettes, cassettes, and machines for backup (and the best-quality hard drive in the first place, of course). A local dealer who sells you the entire package may be willing to handle the installation of your programs, especially the tricky ones. The dealer should also check to make sure that everything is functioning. Waiting another few days to get these services performed is better than finding out the hard way that something isn't working right.

*Williams: How to Repair & Maintain Your Apple Computer (Chilton)*

When you make your own backups, monitor every step of the procedure carefully. In most cases, the program will tell you if it is having troubles with the backup. Then you can take the proper steps to correct the situation.

Installation of the disk hardware is simple; it requires nothing more than inserting the interface card into the peripheral slot of your choice inside the computer and then plugging in the connectors and cables.

The software installation, unfortunately, is not all that simple. If the dealer you bought the unit from won't help, all you can do is follow the instructions provided by the manufacturer meticulously and hope for the best.

Each case is different. There are no general guidelines other than "Be careful!" The way you use your Winchester will be different from the way someone else uses his or hers. Your programs are likely to be different. (Some programs will not load onto a hard drive without some effort on your part; a few won't transfer at all.)

The hard drive is an important part of a system. Don't take the installation lightly. Imagine losing all the programs and data on a single diskette—multiply that by about 30 and you'll have an idea of how devastating Winchester problems can be.

## PRINTERS

Printers come in two basic types and configurations. The two types are dot matrix and wheel or ball printers (letter-quality printers). The two configurations are parallel and serial. A serial printer uses data that is sent one bit at a time. A parallel printer uses data that is sent one byte (eight bits) at a time. Each has advantages and disadvantages. Most people use the parallel configuration since this leaves open the serial connectors for other functions, such as modem communications.

Cabling is the biggest consideration in the installation of a printer. If you try to build your own cable, it can get very complicated. Fortunately, the Apple is so popular that finding the proper cable for any printer should be easy.

Before even attempting to make any connections, get out the manual for your printer and read it cover to cover. Become familiar with the operations, options, switch settings, and so forth. The more you know, the better.

Visually inspect the printer. Locate the controls and learn how to use them—even if you don't think you'll need those options. Also look at the print head. Some are tied in place to reduce damage in shipping. Others may be packed along the sides.

As with many computer devices, printers usually have DIP switches to set.

*Williams: How to Repair & Maintain Your Apple Computer (Chilton)*

The printer was designed and built to accommodate a variety of computers. The switches allow you to configure the printer to your needs. The switches may also set other functions of the printer. Don't forget to shut down the power before changing any of the DIP switch settings. Most printers won't recognize switch setting changes while power flows. Others can be permanently damaged.

The manual that came with the printer should tell you everything you need to know about the switch settings. Read it carefully. You can't damage anything by not adjusting the settings properly, but the printer won't operate correctly, if it works at all.

## MODEMS

Two basic types of modems are currently available, internal and external. Both work equally well, and each has its own advantages and disadvantages. Installation of either is as simple as plugging in a few cords.

The internal modem is generally less expensive because it doesn't require some of the circuitry of the external type. It also tucks inside the computer and out of the way. Your desk is less cluttered, and there are fewer wires strung about. The internal modem also eliminates the need (and expense) for an asynchronous (serial) port card. This won't be important if you already have a serial port available, but if you don't have one, the expense of an external modem goes up even more.

The major disadvantage of the internal modem is that you can't move it from computer to computer. If you have more than one computer, or if you decide to buy another, the modem is basically stuck where it is.

A less significant disadvantage is that the internal type takes up one of the slots in the computer.

An external modem has the advantage of being portable. You can move it from computer to computer merely by changing the cables. The controls are on the modem, making it easier to handle and monitor.

The primary disadvantage is cost. The modem itself costs more usually. If you don't already have an asynchronous port, you'll have to buy one. If this is the case, you are still using up another slot in the computer. (A multifunction card can usually take care of this.)

An external modem may be *direct connect* or *acoustic*. Acoustic modems have been in use for many years but are now essentially obsolete. They have the advantage of being very inexpensive. These modems have a cradle for the telephone. The computer generates beeps to represent data; the beeps are picked up by the telephone in the same way that your voice and other sounds are. Acoustic modems have a severe disadvantage. As they pick up the beeps that are the data, they also pick up any other sounds in the room. This can produce garbled or unusable data. The poorer the fit of the telephone receiver into the cradle, the more garbage that will be picked up from the room.

Direct-connect modems eliminate this problem and are generally preferred. A line connects the modem directly to the telephone outlet in the wall. No external sounds can invade.

Both internal and external modems come in two speeds; 300 and 1,200 baud, with one baud being one bit per second. For example, a 300-baud modem will transmit and receive data at 300 bits per second. The 1,200-baud modem is four times faster, making it generally better. However, it's also much more expensive.

Many modems that handle 1,200 baud can be switched to handle slower speeds. A computer that uses this kind of modem can communicate with other computers that use only the slower models. A modem that cannot make this change will save you only $150 (or less). You cannot work a 300-baud modem at 1,200.

The usual upper limit for reliability across standard telephone lines is 1,200 baud. At speeds higher than this, the quality of data transmission and reception drops, often resulting in garbled and unusable data.

If you're planning to hook up a modem, two excellent reference books are available. For review of communications software, see *A Critic's Guide to Software for the Apple* and *Apple-Compatible Computers*. For more information about modems, installation of serial peripherals, and direct computer-to-computer communications links, see *Increasing Your Effectiveness Through Computer Communications*. Both books were written by Phillip Good and published by Chilton Book Company.

## MULTIFUNCTION BOARDS

A multifunction board is any accessory board that provides more than one feature, such as RAM and a serial port. These boards have found great popularity with computer users because of the limited number of slots inside the cabinet. The typical setup for the Apple takes up one of the eight slots right away (for drive controller cards), which leaves only seven slots to handle an abundance of other possibilities. A multifunction card can take care of more than one job and will take up only one expansion slot.

The more popular multifunction boards have RAM, one or more serial ports, one or more parallel ports, and a clock-calendar. Multifunction cards that carry RAM come with print spoolers and RAM disks. RAM boards will work only in slot 0, unless they are designed to be RAM drive boards.

Installing these boards can be complicated, but with a little common sense you can install one without difficulty.

As always, begin by reading through the instructions completely. Don't skim past sections just because you think you won't be needing them. You simply can't know too much about the board and its features.

If you're not careful when installing a new multifunction card, you can run into all sorts of problems. The two most common are conflicts in memory and hardware settings. If your system functioned perfectly before the installation and suddenly something isn't working any more, chances are you've missed a switch setting or are trying to get the computer to do something it can't.

Since options on the Apple are accessed via port numbers, some multifunction cards use ports that should be empty (i.e., ghost ports) to select an option. In the IIe, for example, the 80-column card in the expansion slot acts as if it is in slot 3, even though it is not. It even overrides anything that is in slot 3.

Some RAM boards require modifications to the mother board. Other times, a RAM chip must be removed from the mother board and placed on the card. This is done to make it easy for the computer to switch banks from the mother board to the expansion card. Sometimes you must set switches on the card itself.

There can be more than 64K on the Apple. The IIe, for example, has 64K on the mother board and can have 64K on the extended 80-column card as well. Bank switching allows RAM to be mapped on top of RAM. A soft switch or other means is used to select which bank (1K, 16K, 64K, or another size segment) is meant when the RAM's address is specified. Follow the instructions that come with the expansion card very carefully.

Many people find that accessories that worked correctly before adding to the system no longer work after. In such cases, the problem is often caused by one piece of hardware interfering with another. Other problems result from the program's using "standard" slots for devices. For example, many programs expect the disk drive card to be in slot 6 and the printer in slot 1. A multifunction card that does too many things might be incompatible with the programs you are using.

These conflicts can result in what appears to be malfunctions, such as the computer or the attached devices refusing to work. Before you suspect the hardware, make sure that you've eliminated any conflicts between the installed devices.

A simple example occurs when an 80-column board is inserted in slot 0 on the IIe. Programs that use PR#3 select the ROM of the card in slot 3. The ROM of an 80-column board will take over, even if it is in slot 0 and you have specified the card in slot 3. Thus, with an 80-column card in slot 0, it is not possible to use a card with a built-in ROM in slot 3. This causes a ROM address conflict, and most cards will not work.

The software and hardware documentation should give you all the information you need regarding board requirements for port and slot assignments. Check both carefully.

It's possible that the board you choose will not be compatible with your system or with certain devices in your system. The dealer should be able to tell you what you need to know about compatibility. (The easiest way to avoid this problem is to use only name products that have been proved fully compatible.)

## NETWORKING

Networking computers is becoming more and more popular. This method allows several computer stations to share devices (i.e., the individual computers are all connected to a single device). For example, various stations might share a hard drive that contains all the programs and data needed by each station. This plan saves each station an expensive purchase of a hard drive for each computer.

## SOFTWARE

Although the programs you use are not actually devices, there is often an installation procedure to follow. The software manual should give you all the information you need to get the program up and working.

Some software is designed to work on a variety of computers. The manual might contain several sections, each for a different computer. If this is the case, be sure that you're using the one for your Apple.

If the program allows it, make at least one backup copy (preferably two) before you begin. Then if you make a mistake, you're covered.

## SHIFT KEY MODIFICATION FOR THE II AND II+

The IIe allows both upper- and lowercase for keyboard entry. The II and II+ allow only uppercase input. Fortunately, an easy modification to the hardware of your II and II+ will allow many software packages to give you both upper- and lowercase input.

This modification changes the signal on pin 4 of the game I/O socket. Then the software, such as a word processing program, will check the status on this pin. When the signal is high, the character is left in its uppercase state. If the signal on pin 4 is low, the character is converted to lowercase.

For this modification, you'll need a Phillips screwdriver, a soldering iron, and a piece of insulated wire about 18 inches long. The best type of wire for this is the small wire used to wire-wrap computer boards, but almost anything will do. A wire-wrapping tool will also be helpful.

With the power off and the power supply disconnected, remove all peripheral cards from the computer. Next remove the case and disconnect the keyboard cable. Follow the instructions from Chapter 5 and remove the mother board.

Strip away about $\frac{1}{2}$ inch of insulation from each end of the wire. This goes to pin 4 (fourth pin from the bottom left when viewed from underside) of the game I/O and to the bottom of the mother board. If you have a wire-wrap tool, use it to attach the wire to the pin (see Figure 8–1). Otherwise, make a loop in

**FIG. 8–1**   Attaching the wire to pin 4 of the game I/O.

*Williams: How to Repair & Maintain Your Apple Computer (Chilton)*

the wire near the insulation and slide this over the pin. Clip off any excess bare wire with wire cutters. Solder the wire to the pin. Keep in mind the three-second rule so as to prevent damage. Be very careful to apply solder *only* to pin 4 and the wire. Check once more to be sure that everything is as it should be and that the wire is touching pin 4 and only pin 4.

Before reinstalling the mother board, wrap the wire around the plastic snap connector on the bottom right corner. This will help keep the wire from sticking out and will make the job neat. Now you can reinstall the mother board.

At this point, you should determine which keyboard you have. The older keyboards are made of one piece. Newer boards are in two pieces, the mechanical assembly and the encoder board.

With the older keyboard, the other end of the wire goes to pin 2 of the 74LS00 IC chip (U4) located under the space bar of the keyboard. Look at this chip and you'll see a small hole in the top of the module. The pin closest to this hole is pin 1. If the hole isn't there, look for the notch on the chip. Pin 1 is to the left of the notch. Either way you find pin 1, pin 2 is the next one in line.

On the newer keyboard, connect the wire to pin 2 (second pin from the right as shown in Figure 8–2) of the long connector pins on the keyboard mechanical assembly. You can also make the connection with the single solder lead located in the boxed-in section of the encoder board (see Figure 8–2).

Put everything back together again carefully. Load the computer with software that can detect the shift key module. Lowercase should now show up.

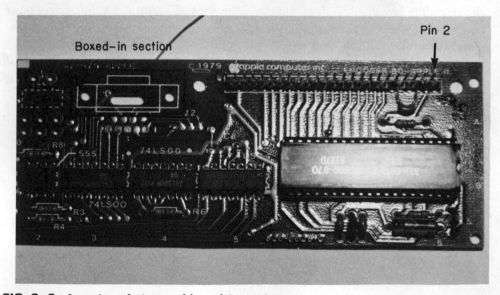

**FIG. 8–2**   Location of pin 2 and boxed-in section.

*Williams: How to Repair & Maintain Your Apple Computer (Chilton)*

## OTHER ADDITIONS

There is very little that the Apple can't do if you install the proper devices. It can pretend to be a different computer through use of an emulation package. It can become an artist or draftsman with the installation of a plotter.

For some accessories, installation is as easy as attaching a cable. Others require special patches to the software (either to the software that comes with the device, to the DOS, or possibly to both). A few devices require custom-written software.

The dealer should be able to inform you of the difficulty in installing a particular device. Part of the sale is to provide to the customer (free or at a reasonable price) the initial assistance needed for the installation, special software or software patching programs, and whatever else is needed.

## SUMMARY

Adding options and devices to your system is usually simple enough for the typical user to handle. Getting a new monitor to work is merely a matter of plugging it in (to the proper type of adapter board). A multifunction card requires that you set a few switches but essentially is a "plug in and go" circumstance.

A few items, such as a complex network, demand special knowledge. Even installing a hard drive can present problems if you're doing it for the first time.

Before purchasing any device you plan to install yourself, you should know the difficulty involved. Before beginning the installation, read the instructions completely. Then go through the installation steps in your head. Do you understand what to do, when, and why?

Before you decide to give up, read through the instructions again. Most of the time the information you need is right there—if you take the time to dig it out.

# Dealing with the
# Technician
# 9

No matter how well you maintain your computer or how much you learn about repairing it, sometimes you will have no choice but to call in a professional (and pay those professional fees!). It can't be helped. Certain repairs demand the use of special, expensive equipment. Others require special knowledge that is far beyond the scope of any single book.

This book is meant to reduce to a minimum those times when you have to hire a professional and to cut the amount you'll have to spend when those times occur. When you consult a professional, you will already have taken care of many of the steps of diagnosis and will be able to supply a great deal of information to the technician. Since you've spent the time, he or she doesn't have to (and you don't have to pay for the time).

This book can go a long way toward reducing costs, but it can't eliminate them altogether.

## MAIL ORDER

If you purchase through the mail, the situation is different. Very few mail order companies are set up to handle questions or problems. You get a discount price, but you are expected to take care of everything by yourself. The only responsibility that many mail order companies accept is that the equipment is "as advertised." While they do guarantee that the equipment will arrive in good

*Williams: How to Repair & Maintain Your Apple Computer (Chilton)*

condition, they usually assume that the buyer knows enough to get the equipment or software functioning.

There is nothing dishonest in this, and it isn't because the mail order companies don't care. They simply aren't set up in the same way that a local dealer is. They don't have the technical staff on hand to take care of questions and problems. Their basic job is to fill your order, which they usually do quite well.

If you know for certain that you can handle any problems with the installation and that you can wait for the delivery (and the delivery of the exchange if this is needed), mail order can save you some money.

If you have any doubts about your technical knowledge, you are probably better off working with a local dealer.

## DEALER RESPONSIBILITIES

When selling you equipment or software, the dealer assumes a certain amount of responsibility. (If the dealer doesn't, you should probably find another.) The first dealer responsibility is to make sure that the computer is functioning when you get it. If you're buying an entire system, the dealer should see that everything functions as a unit before turning it over to you. It should not be handed over as a pile of boxes. If the dealer operates this way, you might as well go through a mail order company and save some money. Insist that product support promises are put in writing.

The Apple is quite versatile. It will accept a wide variety of options manufactured by nearly as many companies. Attainment of this versatility sometimes requires adjustments. Whether these are handled in the equipment (through DIP switches or some other way) or the software, the dealer should take care of all the little details for you.

Many dealers include training in the purchase price. This training isn't meant to make you a computer expert—that takes years of work. The purpose of this training is to get you familiar with the computer and the software. (Unfortunately, a lot of the training simply does what the documentation should have done in the first place.)

Occasionally the dealer will charge a small fee for training. This is often true for instruction in how to operate a complicated piece of software. Even a $1,000 software program doesn't automatically bring with it a complete course, however. The dealer's responsibility is to show you the basics required. Preferably, when you walk out the door with the package under your arm, it should be ready to stick into the drive of your computer without the hassle of initializing and installing. (Bring or buy some blank diskettes. If you wish the dealer to install the system on the diskette, also bring along your own copy of DOS. It is technically illegal for anyone but you to put DOS onto a diskette.)

After you purchase either hardware or software, the dealer continues to have the responsibility of customer care. If you have a problem a few weeks or months after getting the equipment home, you should feel welcome to call in with questions, even after the warranty has expired.

Manufacturers of both hardware and software are famous for refusing to talk to the end user. End-user dealings are usually assumed by them to be the responsibility of the person who sold you the item. Thus, even if it is not wanted, the responsibility often falls on the dealer to provide customers with the needed information.

People who are new to computing (about 75% of the dealer's sales) won't know what questions to ask when they make a purchase. Something as simple as formatting a diskette is a major accomplishment for some newcomers. The more the buyer works with the computer, the more questions he or she will have. (After a short time, certain questions and problems are bound to come up.)

**FIG. 9–1**  The computer store.

*Williams: How to Repair & Maintain Your Apple Computer (Chilton)*

The dealer should provide competent technical assistance after the sale. The user needs a source of information; this includes both technical questions involving operation of the software and hardware purchased and repair when something goes wrong.

Simple questions should be without charge (if you're a customer). Questions that involve some instruction or other lengthy personal attention will probably require a fee. Repairs of any size will cost unless you're under warranty or have a service contract (which also costs).

Some dealers work on a smaller basis and do not keep a technical staff in the shop. If this is the case, the dealer should at least be able to guide you to the proper people or find the answers to your questions. Being small is no excuse for being unable to provide customer service when it is needed. Customer service is the responsibility of dealers of any size and something you should look for when choosing a dealer.

## YOUR RESPONSIBILITIES

If you expect assistance or information from a local dealer, you should begin by giving that dealer some business. If you bought your computer through the mail, don't expect the local dealer to answer all your questions and take care of all your problems free of charge.

Even if you didn't purchase your system from a particular dealer, you can build a working relationship by giving the company other business. The next time you're in the market for a printer, a monitor, or software, stop in and see the dealer you plan to use for help. You might have been thinking about getting some training on how to operate one of your programs. Perhaps the dealer has a course available.

## THE TECHNICIAN

With the information in this book, you should be able to provide a considerable amount of information to the technician. Your goals are to reduce the cost of repair and the amount of time that repair will take. You'll be gaining a secondary benefit in that you'll be letting the technical staff know that you have some idea of what you're talking about.

Before even calling, try to find out if the malfunction has been caused by operator error. Unfortunately, the technician is probably used to dealing with customers who haven't even bothered to read the instruction manual.

The more accurate the information you provide, the easier the job of the

*Williams: How to Repair & Maintain Your Apple Computer (Chilton)*

technician. To you this means increased efficiency, lower cost, and less down-time with your computer sitting on the testing bench. If the technician (and the shop) is honest and reliable, just the knowledge that they're dealing with some-one intelligent will help. If the shop happens to be one of the very few dishon-est ones around, the fact that you know a little something can deter the tech-nician from trying to pull a fast one.

If you're observant, you can tell quite a bit about how well the technician "knows his stuff" even over the phone. His or her responses to your information should make sense. (At the same time, a response of "I can't tell without looking at it" is often legitimate.) The technician should be able to answer your ques-tions without tossing around unnecessary technical jargon. If you have any qualms about the technician's qualifications, ask.

Don't be afraid to make suggestions or helpful comments. It's possible that you know something special about the circumstances. If you've gathered infor-mation (perhaps from the tests you've performed from this book), offer it. Any-thing that makes the technician's job easier will be appreciated. And it may also help reduce the amount you pay for the technical work.

## REPAIR TERMS

Two-way communication is important in any transaction. Both parties should understand fully what is promised and what is expected before things begin. Misunderstandings can come up all too easily unless anticipated before things start.

You should have some idea of the terms and the cost before the work begins. The shop may not be able to give you an exact price until they've found the problem. (For example, a problem that you think is something minor in the disk drive might be something major on the system board.)

An experienced technician will usually be able to give you a fairly accurate estimate. This should be given to you in writing before the actual work begins. If further testing and diagnosis reveal that the problem is something more expensive, be sure to have it in writing that the dealer will call you before going ahead (unless you don't care about the expense).

Along with the price estimate you should have a time estimate. How long will your computer be tied up? If it goes beyond this period can you get a "loaner" or at least rent a machine to use while you're waiting?

What kind of warranty is given with the work? (It should be *at least* 30 days on both parts and labor.) Getting the warranty in writing is important.

When the work is completed, ask for an itemized bill. This is your protection for any warranty service and is also a good thing to have around for future reference. To avoid complications, you should request the itemized list before the work begins. Some shops automatically keep itemized lists. Others don't.

Before turning over the computer, be sure that the technician knows as much as possible about the problem, including the symptoms. If not, he or she may not know where to begin or what to look for. The more information you can provide, the better.

Communication is important if you wish maximum efficiency and a good repair job.

## SOLVING PROBLEMS

No matter how good the technician or how reputable the company, problems will arise. Many could be prevented if communication between you and the shop were carried on properly to begin with. Others result from unforeseen malfunctions; perhaps one of the parts installed is faulty. Occasionally a mistake will have been made during repair.

If the work is not done to your satisfaction, say so. But keep in mind that the nastier you are, the less willing they'll be to take care of the problem.

Talk to the technician who did the work first. Chances are the problem is something he or she can handle. If not, go to the service manager and then to the general manager. It might take a little longer to go through the chain of command, but the end results are often better.

## SUMMARY

Before making a purchase, determine whether you'll be able to handle the installation alone, without the advice of a local dealer. If so, you can save money by using a mail order company. If you have doubts, you might be better off going with a local dealer.

Both the dealer and you have responsibilities. It's a two-way street—or should be. The dealer owes the customers all the necessary support for whatever is being sold and should be willing to stand behind the products carried. The staff should be competent enough to give sensible advice as to which products will best suit your needs.

*Williams: How to Repair & Maintain Your Apple Computer (Chilton)*

# The IIc
# 10

When the first Apple computers were made available to the public, a precedent was set. Never before was the operation of a computer quite so easy and friendly. The user didn't need a degree in computer science to get the benefits of a computer.

One of the primary ideas behind those first Apples, and all Apple computers through the IIe, was that the user should be able to handle most repairs quickly and easily and make the system into whatever is desired. The top of the machine merely flipped out of the way. The boards all slid into place easily. Even the mother board was attached in such a way that it could be removed with little effort.

This was a trial period for personal computing. It didn't take the designers at Apple long to realize that certain things were being used by virtually everyone who had one of the Apple computers.

Along came the new line of Apples, including the IIc. All major functions are built in; none are added by the end users. New manufacturing techniques have made the already-reliable components even more reliable. Even the number of components has been reduced (from 110 in the IIe to only 40 in the IIc). The need for the user to get inside the computer has been removed.

Unlike previous models, the IIc has a cabinet that is not meant to be opened by the end user. In fact, doing so automatically voids the warranty. This should be no problem, since there is literally nothing inside that the user can

*Williams: How to Repair & Maintain Your Apple Computer (Chilton)*

**FIG. 10–1**  The Apple IIc. *Courtesy of Apple Computer, Inc.*

fix. There are no expansion cards and no plug-in components. The 40 ICs inside
the IIc are soldered into place, not socketed.

One of the main reasons for soldered rather than socketed chips is to provide stability. The IIc is designed to be portable. It even has a built-in carrying
handle (which doubles as a tilting support arm for the computer); it is small
enough to fit inside most briefcases. Sockets make changing components easy.
They also make it easy for chips to work loose as the computer is moved from
place to place. The IIc's soldering ensures that the chips and other components
remain secure.

The IIc is designed to be repaired by what Apple calls "Level 1 Service."
This means that even the trained technician performs repairs by replacement.

*Williams: How to Repair & Maintain Your Apple Computer (Chilton)*

If the mother board, or any part of the mother board, goes bad, the entire mother board is swapped for a new one. If the drive analog card, or any component on it, is faulty, the entire card is changed.

This is meant to be. Although it might sound like a poor way to design a computer, under the circumstances this method is quite efficient and not much more expensive than repairing by component replacement. The reason is that the faulty board has a trade-in value. Some shops will also charge a modest technical fee to make the swap, but the cost will not include possibly hours of work spent in trying to track the problem to a single component.

The danger of plugging a device into the wrong slot has been reduced. The back panel has little pictures to show you what each port does. The cable that connects the port and the device contains the corresponding picture. Unlike with other computers, it is virtually impossible to damage the computer by connecting something incorrectly.

## SPECIFICATIONS

The IIc comes with 128K of RAM and 16K of ROM built in. This should be enough to handle almost any need and is twice the RAM available on the stock IIe. The CPU is a newly designed 65C02, operating at 1.02MHz.

A single half-height disk drive (5¼ inch, soft sector) is built in. You can add one more drive merely by plugging it into the 19-pin D-shell port in the back (marked with a picture of a diskette). The main drive and the external one both have a 140K storage capacity. A small part of this is used by the operating system. With ProDOS or Pascal, for example, 137K is left open to the user. With standard DOS, 124K is available.

Two serial ports are available. These can run just about any two serial devices you wish to use (such as a serial printer or plotter and a modem). One port is marked with a little telephone. The other is marked with a picture of a printer. There are no parallel ports.

There are two video ports. A 15-pin D-shell connector allows you to attach a standard television set, an RGB monitor, or an optional flat LCD display predicted to be available in late 1984. Next to this is a standard RCA plug, for connection to almost any monochrome or color monitor.

A 9-pin connector allows the attachment of a hand-controlled device. This can be a joystick, hand-controlled paddles, or a mouse.

The power supply accepts line voltage between 105 and 125 volts AC at 60 Hz. The small 25-watt power supply can be bypassed by using an optional 12-volt power pack. This option ($39 at time of this writing) plus the optional liquid crystal display (LCD) allow total portability. You can even plug the computer into the cigarette lighter of your car.

The keyboard has a membrane beneath the key caps. This reduces the danger of severe damage caused by spills. It also makes changing the keyswitches, which are soldered into place, a bit tricky. You still should keep all liquids away from the computer. The keyboard shifts from standard to DVORAK configuration.

Operating temperature for the IIc should be 10°C to 40°C (50°F to 104°F); relative humidity 0% to 90%.


## DISASSEMBLY

If you ever decide to open the cabinet of the IIc (and again, there really isn't much need to), do so very carefully. It is an easy job, but one that can cause expensive troubles.

There are ten screws on the bottom of the cabinet (Figure 10-2)—six to hold the main cabinet in place and four in the center hold the drive in place. Don't remove those four until after the cabinet has been taken off.

At the back of the computer is a flat plastic panel. This panel marks the various ports available and allows access to those ports. Before you can separate the top half of the cabinet from the bottom, the panel has to be removed (Figure 10-3).

This can be tricky. The key is to move slowly and carefully, while paying attention every step of the way. The panel is held in place by small plastic prongs. These can be broken all too easily. For each one you snap off, the panel becomes less secure and less stable.

Once the panel is out of the way, lift the front of the top half of the cabinet. It should now lift off easily. If it doesn't, don't force it. As with the back panel, you could cause damage.

Inside the cabinet (Figure 10-4), the drive is covered by a metal shield. This slides into place and locks against the front of the computer. The drive is held secure by the four screws through the bottom of the cabinet. After these are removed, it lifts out easily. Underneath you'll find the mother board (Figure 10-5), which is also held in place by screws.

Within just a few minutes the entire computer can be disassembled into its parts: the three-piece cabinet, the drive shield, the drive, the power supply, the mother board, and the keyboard. If you went this far, you'd realize just how little maintenance and repair are required and why even trained technicians merely swap the offending board instead of trying to replace individual components.

*Williams: How to Repair & Maintain Your Apple Computer (Chilton)*

**FIG. 10–2** The bottom of the IIc.

## SOFTWARE PROBLEMS

The IIc is designed to run most of the software that can work with the IIe. There are a few exceptions to this, so if you wish to buy software for a IIc, be sure to find out if the program is compatible. (It's a good idea to make sure that the program can be returned if it doesn't work with your IIc.)

There are several reasons why a program may work with the IIe and not the IIc. The CPU of the IIe is the same 6502 that is used in the rest of the II series. The IIc uses a 65C02, which is a modified version with 27 more internal instructions than the 6502.

Although the IIe and IIc both have 16K of ROM, the IIc ROM is different. The IIc has 80-column capability built in, which is handled by the ROM. Apple

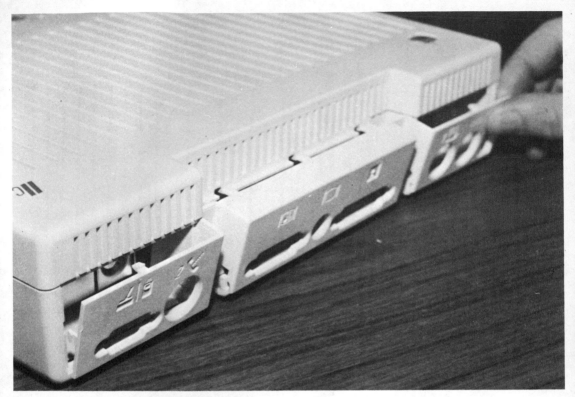

**FIG. 10–3**   Removing the rear panel.

computers through the IIe use an expansion board, not the ROM, for this function.

Another possible conflict is caused by the drive used. The IIc uses a half-height drive. While the specifications for this drive are nearly identical to those of the full-sized drives used by other computers in the II series (48 TPI, 35 tracks, etc.), the full-sized drives have one capability that the half-height drives do not.

One protection scheme used to prevent software pirating was to record certain information between the standard tracks. For example, an important piece of data needed to operate a program might be placed *between* tracks 3 and 4, with instructions built into the program to tell the read head of the drive to go to this spot. Those instructions are still there, of course, but the half-height drive cannot obey them.

*Williams: How to Repair & Maintain Your Apple Computer (Chilton)*

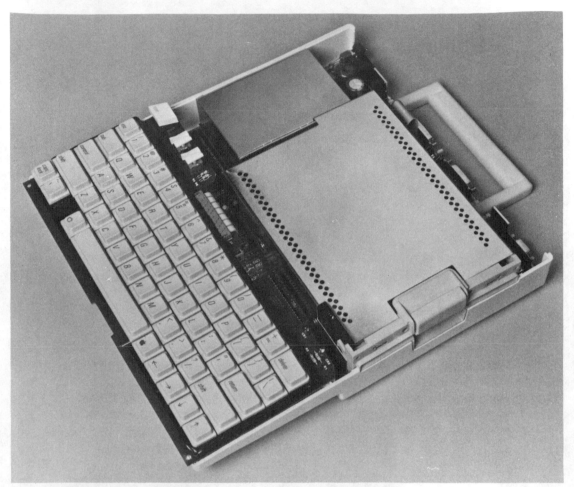

**FIG. 10—4**   Inside the cabinet. *Courtesy of Apple Computer, Inc.*

The program may also have the RAM mapped in a way that cannot be used by the IIc. This is because of the way the 65C02 CPU gets at the built-in RAM. A IIe comes with 64K. For it to access additional RAM requires memory mapping.

These differences add some power to the IIc. They also make certain programs cough and choke. Before you suspect or blame the computer or drive, try the same program on a IIe. This will tell you if the program is the cause of the trouble. If it functions perfectly on the IIe, then either that program is not com-

*Williams: How to Repair & Maintain Your Apple Computer (Chilton)*

**FIG. 10–5** The IIc mother board. *Courtesy of Apple Computer, Inc.*

patible with the IIc or something is wrong with your IIc computer. To find out which is the case, load in a program that you know is good. If another program works in your IIc, then the problem is simply incompatibility and is nothing to worry about.

Unfortunately, the IIc will not handle any programs that use CP/M as the operating system. However, many manufacturers of Apple software that uses CP/M are currently redesigning these packages so that they will work. And a number of new programs are being designed strictly for the IIc to make use of the added power available.

## DIAGNOSIS

Most of the rules for diagnosis of problems and many of the cures are the same for all computers. Even if you have a IIc and not one of the other computers in the II series, read through the rest of this book.

A revised version of the diagnostics diskette should be available soon. The existing program (or the one that came with this book if you bought it as part of a package) will still perform certain tests for the IIc. Most notable is the drive speed test (M). Adjustment, if needed, is made with a thin blade through a tiny access hole on the bottom of the cabinet. Without the diagnostics diskette, you would probably not want to attempt to make this adjustment.

Almost everything is built into the IIc. The only additions are the things that plug into it. Because of the design of the IIc, spotting the source of a malfunction is easy. It can be in one of three places only: the mother board, the connecting cable, or the external device. It's a simple process of elimination.

A blank monitor could mean that the monitor is faulty or is not receiving a signal. (Don't forget to check for the obvious. Is the monitor plugged in and turned on? Is the cable attached?) Use a meter to test the cable for continuity. As described earlier in the book, this is merely a matter of touching the black probe to one end of the cable, and the red probe to the same wire at the opposite end.

Testing the monitor and mother board is simple. You can either plug the monitor into another computer or plug your own computer into another monitor. (You can also attach the IIc to a standard television set. The IIc has a built-in RF modulator.) Either way you'll have found the source of trouble. If your monitor works with another computer (and the cable has tested fine), the problem has to be in your mother board. If your computer correctly drives another monitor, then your monitor is the problem, not the computer.

The same steps can be followed to test all external devices. The IIc is portable enough (just a little more than seven pounds) to carry to the shop if you don't have immediate access to another of the device you suspect. The testing will take just a few minutes.

## SUMMARY

The IIc was designed to fulfill several needs. The compact simplicity of the design means less need for maintenance and repair. The typical user needs to do little other than follow the normal maintenance routines (see Chapter 7) required for all computers.

The high degree of portability is made possible by the small size and is made secure by the use of soldering rather than sockets to hold all components in place. The optional power pack increases portability. When the LCD becomes available, few other computers will be able to boast of the same portability without sacrifice of power.

With 128K of on-board RAM, the tiny IIc has plenty of memory. Since memory is built in, there are no memory-mapping errors associated with adding memory later on.

Although the IIc can run most of the existing software written for the IIe, some programs may be incompatible because of differences in the CPU, the ROM, RAM mapping, and the way the disk drive works. Keep in mind that if a program refuses to run, it may be nothing more than incompatibility.

There is very little that the end user can do as far as repair is concerned. The IIc is designed to eliminate the need for repair. Even though instructions are given in this chapter on how to disassemble the IIc, it is generally not a good idea to try. Since repair is by replacement, and since replacement in the IIc is such a simple matter, the technician's charge for repair will most likely be small and hardly worth the risk of causing damage to the cabinet or devices.

====================================

# The Diagnostics
# Diskette
# 11

If you bought this book as part of a package, you have a diagnostics diskette ready to help you spot possible troubles. If you have the nondisk version of the book, you can obtain a diagnostics disk at your local computer store. (*Computer Checkup*, available from Software Publishing Corporation, 1901 Landings Drive, Mountain View, CA 94043, is an excellent diagnostics tool.)

The diagnostic routines work with the Apple II, II+, and IIe. Some tests will also run with the IIc. The idea behind this program is not only to help you spot trouble but also to keep you informed of the general operating integrity of your system. Running the program should be a regular part of your maintenance. I suggest you read the basic diagnostic steps in Chapter 2 again before beginning.

Operating the program is quite easy. It is menu driven and gives you instructions every step of the way. You can also refer to this chapter if you need additional help.

## GETTING STARTED

Before loading the diskette, cover the write-protect notch. This will protect you in case you make any mistakes (assuming that the write-protect switch is functioning properly). After this, put the diagnostics diskette in drive 1 and turn on the power. After a few seconds you'll get a main menu, (see Figure 11–1).

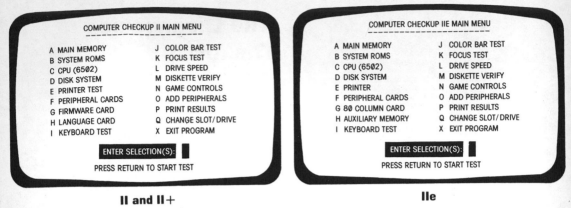

II and II+                                             IIe

**FIG. 11–1**  The main menu.

If you're using the diskette for the first time, you'll need to set up the diskette to test for the options and cards you have installed. To do this, choose F, PERIPHERAL CARDS, and press RETURN.

This test (Figure 11–2 shows the test screen) does two things. Later on it will allow you to test the cards you have installed (details for this are in the "Peripheral Cards Test" section of this chapter). If you're installing the diskette to meet your individual needs, this test generates the needed five-digit signature codes that allow the program to identify and test the boards you have.

To generate signature codes, the program puts out signals to the cards as it searches through the expansion slots. How a particular card receives and sends back the signal determines what the signature is. Two cards that appear iden-

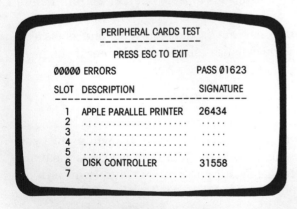

**FIG. 11–2**  Peripheral cards test screen.

*Williams: How to Repair & Maintain Your Apple Computer (Chilton)*

tical, such as the parallel printer card in your computer and that card in your friend's computer, can generate completely different signature codes.

The first time you run this routine, and any time you run it to make changes in the cards you have installed, the write-protect notch must be uncovered. The signature codes are stored on the diagnostics diskette. As soon as you've completed the initial setup or changes, cover the write-protect notch to protect yourself against accidental erasure.

Selecting F and pressing RETURN will begin this routine. Jot down the name of the card and the signature code generated in a convenient place. When you run the test in the future, you'll be comparing the code generated then with this original signature code. See "Peripheral Cards Test" in this chapter for more information.

After you've set up the program to suit your individual needs and have written down the names of the expansion cards and their signature codes, press ESC.

## RUNNING THE TESTS

For regular maintenance checks, you'll want to run more than one test. Other times you'll want to check a particular device or run a test numerous times. This diagnostics program gives you the choice.

To run the tests in sequence with the program automatically moving from one test to the next, type in the letters of all the tests you wish to run. (Be sure to type them in order.) When you're finished, press RETURN and the program will take it from there.

If a problem shows up, make a note of it. Later you can go back and run that test individually. You may also wish to run a single test, perhaps numerous times, if you suspect a problem in a certain device. To do this, merely press the letter for the test required and RETURN. Only that test will be run. You have complete control over it and can let the test run for several hours to help spot intermittent problems.

The display of most tests is similar. The usual way of stopping the test is to press ESC, which is shown on the screen. Below that and to the left, the number of errors found is shown. To the right of that PASSES shows you how many times that particular test has been run.

The test results can be automatically sent to the printer, which comes in handy if you plan to run the test unattended. A printed copy of the test results can also serve as a guide for the technician, should professional help be needed. All you have to do is to press P before making the test selection. The program will ask, PRINT TEST RESULTS? Y/N. N will take you back to the main menu again. Y will bring up ENTER PRINTER SLOT #. Now all the test results will be sent to the printer, giving you a permanent copy. It's a good idea to store a copy that is made when you know everything is functioning correctly.

Normally, the program looks for the drive controller card to be in slot 6 and assumes that you are using drive 1. Testing drive 2, or testing either drive if the controller card is in a slot other than 6, requires that you take a moment and let the program know. Selection Q allows you to change the drive to be checked, the slot containing the controller card, or both.

After entering a Q, the program will ask you to ENTER SLOT #. The number in parentheses tells you which slot is being used at present for the controller card. (Default is slot 6.) If this number is correct, simply press RETURN. If you wish to change the slot number, press the new number and then RETURN. Be sure that the drive controller is in the slot number you enter, or the program will not be able to run properly (if at all).

Next you'll be asked to ENTER DRIVE #. Again there will be a number in parentheses to identify the drive being accepted as default. Press RETURN to accept this, or enter the new number.

## MAIN MEMORY TEST

Test A checks your computer's RAM. The location of the RAM chips for the II and II+ and for the IIe is shown on the screen. If the chip tests as good, the corresponding spot shows a G. If the chip tests as faulty, that spot shows an asterisk (*) (see Figure 11–3 for sample test screens). This diagram makes it easy

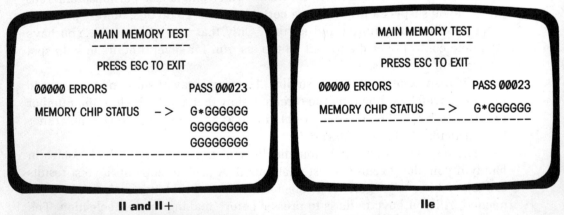

**FIG. 11–3**  Main memory test screens.

*Williams: How to Repair & Maintain Your Apple Computer (Chilton)*

to find out which module has failed (or is failing). For example, if the third spot from the left on the middle row (for the II and II+ test) shows an asterisk (*), the third RAM module from the left on the middle row on the mother board is failing.

An error will be accompanied by one of two error messages. A BANK SELECT ERROR lets you know that the program couldn't access a part of the memory. This could mean that there is something wrong with the mother board. Refer to Chapters 2 and 5. If you haven't found the problem, chances are you'll need a professional technician.

A DATA ERROR AT LOCATION xxxx tells you the specific decimal address of the failure within the RAM module. The normal solution is simply to replace that RAM module.

Testing RAM can be tricky. If you suspect problems with your RAM, select A as an individual test and let it run for at least an hour. This will help catch intermittent problems.

Before giving up, *very carefully* swap modules. For example, if the test shows a particular module as bad, swap this chip with one that was shown as good. The location of the faulty chip should change. It's very important that the two chips are identical. It's even more important that you make the swap carefully. Use a chip extractor, *not* a screwdriver or knife blade. If you can't do it correctly, don't do it at all. Those chips are delicate!

## ROM TEST

The II and II+ have six ROM chips, labeled D0, E0, F0, D8, E8, and F8. The IIe has only two ROM chips, labeled C0 and E0. They are well labeled on the mother board, and the user will see the same labels on the test screen (Figure 11-4). The test is accessed by selecting B from the main menu.

The ROM test will show the chips as either GOOD or BAD. This will appear to the right of the chip label on the screen. If a chip is bad, there will usually be an error message beneath the dashed line (CHECKSUM ERROR is the most common). You don't need to know what this message means; merely copy the message, or run the test results to the printer so you'll have a guide for the technician.

As with the RAM test, if you suspect problems with ROM, select the test individually from the main menu and run the test numerous times. A fail in the test could mean a bad ROM chip. It could also mean that there is a problem in the mother board. Go to Chapters 2 and 5. If this doesn't help, you'll have little choice but to visit a professional.

*Williams: How to Repair & Maintain Your Apple Computer (Chilton)*

```
        SYSTEM ROMS TEST                        SYSTEM ROMS TEST
        -------------                           -------------
        PRESS ESC TO EXIT                       PRESS ESC TO EXIT

00000 ERRORS            PASS 00199     00000 ERRORS            PASS 00025

DØ ROM GOOD        D8 ROM GOOD         CØ ROM GOOD        EØ ROM GOOD
EØ ROM GOOD        E8 ROM GOOD         ----------------------------------
FØ ROM GOOD        F8 ROM GOOD
----------------------------------
```

             **II and II+**                              **IIe**

**FIG. 11-4**   ROM test screens.

## CPU TEST

The II, II+, and IIe use a 6502 CPU. Test C (Figure 11-5 shows a sample test screen) is the same for each. As with the ROM test, the chip is labeled either GOOD or BAD. If it is found bad, return to the test and run it for a number of passes.

Fortunately, the 6502 is one of the least expensive CPUs on the market. It is readily available at many computer stores. If you look around (and call around), you should be able to find one for less than $25.

## DISK DRIVE TEST

This routine tests the disk drives for speed, for writing to the diskette, for reading from the diskette, and for finding data on the diskette (see Figure 11-6 for sample test screen). To run this test, you will need a prepared, blank diskette. This is because the tests will destroy any data on the diskette being used. DO NOT use the diagnostics diskette for this test.

After loading your computer with DOS 3.3, put the blank diskette in drive 1. Then type in INIT HELLO, and press RETURN. This gets the test diskette ready. Label the diskette with something like "Drive Test Diskette Only." Now you can load in the diagnostics diskette, with the write-protect notch covered for protection.

The testing has a time limit of about three minutes, after which it will automatically stop. This is to prevent your power supply from overheating. If you haven't learned what you need to know at the end of the three minutes, give your computer a chance to cool and "rest" before going at it again.

*Williams: How to Repair & Maintain Your Apple Computer (Chilton)*

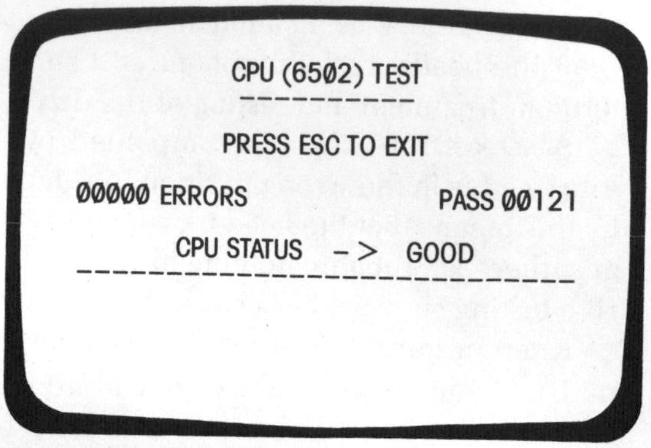

```
        CPU (6502) TEST
        ----------

        PRESS ESC TO EXIT

00000 ERRORS              PASS 00121
        CPU STATUS  - >  GOOD
-----------------------------------
```

**FIG. 11-5**   CPU test screen.

After selecting D, you'll see a display, PUT TEST DISK IN DRIVE 1, SLOT 6." If you wish to test drive 2, or if you have the drive controller card in a slot other than 6, abort the test (by hitting ESC) and select Q to change the drive, slot number, or both, as needed.

When everything is as you need it, replace the diagnostics diskette with the blank test diskette you've prepared. Press any key (other than ESC) to begin.

The speed test checks to see if the drive speed is within .5% of 300 rpm (1.5 rpm, or from 298.5 to 301.5 rpm). Each time it varies beyond this, SPEED ERROR will show. One or two such errors out of many passes is not necessarily bad. The drives will vary in speed slightly. However, you may still wish to check the drive or even adjust its speed. Test L on the diagnostics diskette (see page 185) allows you to test the drive speed more thoroughly and to set it. (See also Chapter 4.)

Read, write, and seek errors can result from a bad diskette, a dirty head, or something more serious. Before disassembling the drive or taking it to some-

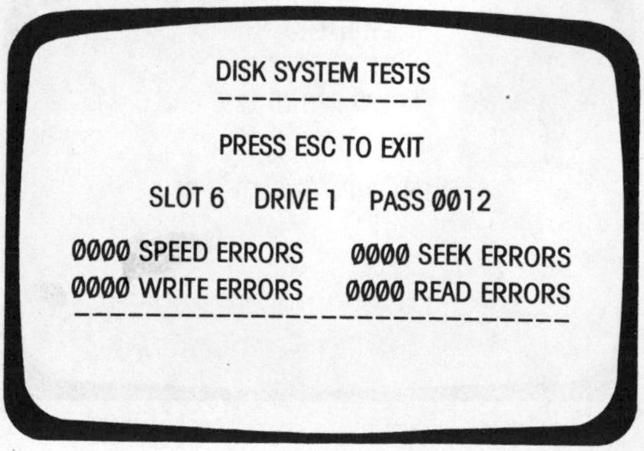

```
        DISK SYSTEM TESTS
        -------------

        PRESS ESC TO EXIT

   SLOT 6   DRIVE 1   PASS 0012

0000 SPEED ERRORS     0000 SEEK ERRORS
0000 WRITE ERRORS     0000 READ ERRORS
--------------------------------------
```

**FIG. 11-6**   Disk drive test screen.

*Williams: How to Repair & Maintain Your Apple Computer (Chilton)*

one for repair, try using another test diskette, maybe even two other diskettes. Clean the heads. If the problems still show up, refer to Chapter 4 for a more thorough treatment and testing of the drive.

A seek error will be accompanied by a beep. This means that the read/ write head is in the wrong position in relation to the tracks of the diskette. Usually this means that the head movement is binding somehow. If it happens only once, there is probably nothing to worry about. If the seek error continues or if drive testing shows other errors, go to Chapter 4.

Keep in mind that if you have found a speed or alignment problem with the drive, you should make copies of all data that was recorded on that drive before making any repairs or adjustments. Use a drive you know is good as the target (the drive containing the diskette on which the data is to be copied), with the suspected drive as the source.

If you make the adjustments before making the copies, you could lose all that data. It may have been recorded according to the maladjustments, and a correctly adjusted drive may not be able to read that data.

## PRINTER TEST

A number of different printers and printer controller cards are available for the Apple. Each will test slightly differently. It's important that you run this test when everything is functioning correctly so that you will have a point of comparison if something goes wrong. Unlike other tests, the printer test does not require you to press RETURN to begin the test. Select E. When the test comes up, merely enter the printer slot number (see Figure 11-7). Be sure the printer is ready and filled with paper.

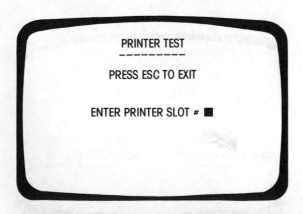

**FIG. 11–7**  Printer test screen.

*Williams: How to Repair & Maintain Your Apple Computer (Chilton)*

The usual printing pattern is diagonal—that is, successive lines contain the same characters starting one place to the left. The letter A, for example, will print in a diagonal line from right to left. All characters should print out in a regular sequence.

Your own printer setup might differ from this. If it does, don't worry unless there is already a problem. Refer to Chapter 6 for more information on printers.

## PERIPHERAL CARDS TEST

You had to perform this step to get the diagnostics diskette running. It should now be set to test the cards you have installed. If you wish to add or take out cards, go to the "Add Peripherals" section in this chapter.

You'll need the list of cards and the signature numbers originally generated when you set up the diagnostics diskette. Enter F to access the test. As it runs, it will regenerate those codes (see Figure 11-8). If they are the same, then the card is fine. If they are different, then something is wrong. (Don't forget that two cards that seem identical may generate slightly different signature codes. If you've changed cards—even cards that seem to be the same—you'll have to go to the "Add Peripherals" section before you can reliably test the cards.)

Some cards will not test correctly. Modem cards and cards that have a clock-calendar are famous for being difficult to test. You may even have to remove these cards before running the test. A changing signature code on such cards does not necessarily indicate that there is a problem.

An asterisk (*) will appear beside those cards that are not generating the same signature each time. If this happens on a standard card, you could be having a problem with that card or perhaps with the slot in which it is inserted.

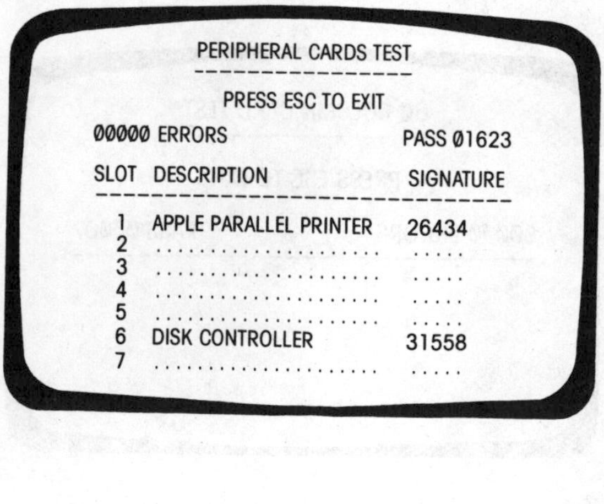

```
            PERIPHERAL CARDS TEST
            -------------------
              PRESS ESC TO EXIT

  00000 ERRORS                    PASS 01623

  SLOT  DESCRIPTION               SIGNATURE
  -----------------------------------------
    1   APPLE PARALLEL PRINTER    26434
    2   ....................      .....
    3   ....................      .....
    4   ....................      .....
    5   ....................
    6   DISK CONTROLLER           31558
    7   ....................      .....
```

**FIG. 11-8**  Peripheral cards test screen.

Williams: How to Repair & Maintain Your Apple Computer (Chilton)

## EIGHTY-COLUMN CARD TEST (IIe)

An 80-column card is helpful if you plan to handle text files. Without this card, everything is displayed in 40 columns. Switching back and forth between 40 columns and 80 is done by soft switches, by the display memory on the card, and by the video circuitry. While the 80-column card test (G) is being run, the normal response is for the screen to show the number of errors to the left and the number of passes to the right (see Figure 11-9). The display should shift back and forth between the two (40-column and 80-column) modes.

## FIRMWARE CARD TEST (II AND II+)

If you have a firmware card installed in your Apple II or II+, you'll have to check certain aspects of the ROM to determine if the ROM chips on the card are functioning properly or not. This test does that for you. It is accessed by selecting G from the main menu.

As with the standard ROM test, the six ROM chips (D0, E0, F0, D8, E8, and F8) are checked. They are labeled either GOOD or BAD (see Figure 11-10). If the test fails, return to the ROM test (page 175 in this chapter). If the ROM chips pass, then chances are the problem is in the firmware card itself.

## ADDED MEMORY TEST (IIe)

This test will determine if the memory portion of the 80-column card is functioning. (Installed RAM on the mother board is covered on page 174.) As with other RAM tests, it is best to let this test run for at least an hour in order to spot intermittent trouble. The auxiliary memory test is option H.

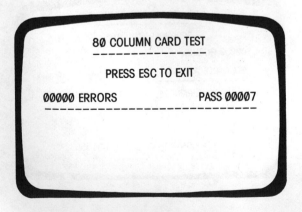

```
        80 COLUMN CARD TEST
        ------------------

          PRESS ESC TO EXIT

00000 ERRORS              PASS 00007
------------------------------------
```

**FIG. 11–9** Eighty-column card test screen.

*Williams: How to Repair & Maintain Your Apple Computer (Chilton)*

```
                    FIRMWARE CARD TEST
                    ------------------

                    PRESS ESC TO EXIT

    00000 ERRORS                    PASS 00103

    D0 ROM GOOD                     D8 ROM GOOD
    E0 ROM GOOD                     E8 ROM GOOD
    F0 ROM GOOD                     F8 ROM GOOD
    ------------------------------------------
```

**FIG. 11-10** Firmware card test screen.

There are eight RAM chips on this expansion card. As with the mother board test, the display shows a G for modules that test as good and an asterisk (*) for modules that fail (see Figure 11-11).

Below the dashed line, you'll see one of two error messages if something is wrong.

You may get a BANK SELECT ERROR. This means that the program could not access a part of the additional RAM installed. The location diagram displayed should show which module is at fault. Try a module swap (carefully) to see if the location changes. If it does, you have found the faulty module. If it doesn't, or if it changes at random, then the problem is elsewhere in that board.

A DATA ERROR AT LOCATION XXXX could again indicate a failing module or a problem deeper in the expansion card. Try to swap the module under suspicion first.

Don't attempt to replace or repair the expansion board before running the RAM test on the main board. The RAM is buffered through the mother board.

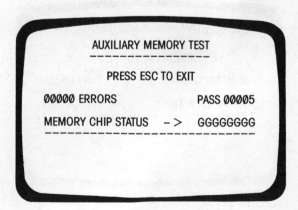

```
                    AUXILIARY MEMORY TEST
                    ---------------------

                    PRESS ESC TO EXIT

    00000 ERRORS                    PASS 00005

    MEMORY CHIP STATUS    - >    GGGGGGGG
    ------------------------------------------
```

**FIG. 11-11** Auxiliary memory test screen.

*Williams: How to Repair & Maintain Your Apple Computer (Chilton)*

What seems to be a problem on the expansion board may have been caused by the mother board.

## LANGUAGE CARD TEST (II AND II+)

You can expand the II or II+ with a language card. The language card test allows you to test the card's RAM. (See also the standard RAM tests detailed on page 174 of this chapter.) There are eight RAM chips on the expansion card, allowing you an additional 16K of RAM. The test shows these, from left to right, and displays either a G for good or an asterisk (*) for bad at each module location (see Figure 11–12). As with other RAM tests, it is best to let this test run for at least an hour in order to catch intermittent or other hard-to-detect problems. Enter an H to get the test ready.

    A BANK SELECT ERROR or a DATA ERROR AT LOCATION XXXX might appear if there is a problem. The first could indicate either a faulty module or an error elsewhere in the board. The second is almost certain to indicate the specific module at fault.

    Be sure to check the main memory before replacing or attempting to repair the expansion board. Since the RAM is buffered here, what seems to be a problem in the expansion memory may actually be caused by a module on the main board

## KEYBOARD TEST

The keyboard test for the II and IIe is essentially the same. The only difference is with the CAPS LOCK key. This must be in the up position on the IIe. The test is

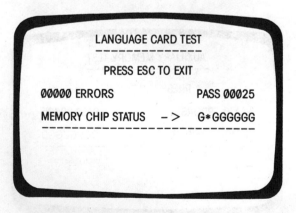

**FIG. 11–12** Language card test screen.

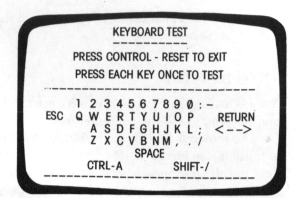

**FIG. 11-13** II and II+ keyboard test screen.

accessed by entering an I from the Main Menu. (See Figures 11–13 and 11–14 for the test screen.)

After this, you merely press each key. The order makes no difference at all, but if you suspect keyboard problems, it is best to pay close attention to which key you are pressing.

As you press the keys, the corresponding character on the screen should disappear. If it doesn't, or if a different character disappears when you press a key, something is wrong. (A beep simply means that you're pressing a key that has already been pressed.)

If you find a problem, the first thing to do is to run the test again to see if you can't isolate the problem to a certain key. Check the cable and all connections. Chapter 6 contains more information on how to check the keyboard and cable.

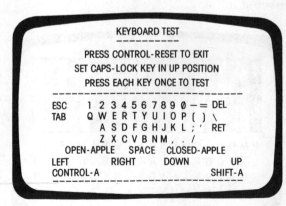

**FIG. 11-14** IIe keyboard test screen.

If everything checks out, the screen will show ALL KEYS FUNCTIONING. To exit the test, press CONTROL-RESET.

## COLOR BAR TEST

Test J does several things. It can be used to test both color and monochrome monitors and to test the computer itself.

The screen is labeled with abbreviations of the colors that are supposed to be present (see Figure 11–15). From left to right, these are black, magenta, dark blue, purple, dark green, gray, medium blue, light blue, brown, orange, gray, pink, green, yellow, aqua, white, black, magenta, dark blue and purple. A monochrome monitor will show the same labels, but of course the bars will be shades of the single color (green, amber, etc.) of the monitor.

If the colors, brightness, and contrast aren't correct, try to make corrections with the controls on the monitor. (You may want to misadjust the monitor while this test is displayed to see what a maladjustment looks like.) Most of the time you'll be able to make the needed adjustments.

If you can't, it's time to refer again to Chapter 2 and to the section covering monitors in Chapter 6. Locating the cause of the trouble is a process of elimination. Try hooking a different monitor to your computer. If the adjustments can now be made, the problem is with your monitor. If they still can't be, the cable or computer is at fault. Eliminate the cable as the cause by testing it for continuity with your VOM.

DO NOT open the monitor and attempt to make internal adjustments unless you know what you are doing. Keep in mind that there is dangerous voltage inside the video display, even after you have turned it off. If you're determined to poke around inside, turn it off and let it sit for several hours or even a full day.

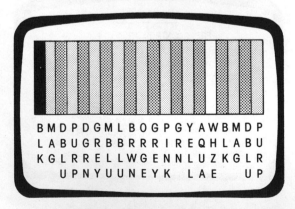

**FIG. 11–15** Color bar test screen.

*Williams: How to Repair & Maintain Your Apple Computer (Chilton)*

## FOCUS TEST

The focus test (selection K) continues the testing of the video portion of your system. The screen (see Figure 11–16) shows a diamond inside a larger rectangle, with a horizontal and vertical line inside the diamond. There are dots at each corner of the rectangle, and four at the center of the screen where the two lines meet.

Everything should be clear and sharp. Some monitors are less sharp than others, so expect slightly different results if you use this test with a different monitor. But all monitors should easily distinguish the lines and dots.

If the lines and dots are not distinguished, try adjusting the controls of your monitor. Contrast and brightness can make the lines and dots appear hazy. If you cannot adjust the monitor, finding the problem is again a process of elimination. Try a different monitor. If it works, the problem is in your own monitor. If it doesn't, test the video cable. The only thing left after eliminating these is the computer itself.

Once again, be extremely careful when working around a monitor. The voltage level inside is potentially deadly and remains even after you've shut off the power. There's little reason to open it, but if you must, do so with great caution.

## DRIVE SPEED TEST

This is another test that should be run regularly as a part of routine maintenance. It will help you keep track of how well your drives are operating. In test D, you checked for drive speed tolerance. That test determined if the speed was within a .5% tolerance of the normal 300 rpm. Any speed between 298.5 and 301.5 earned a passing score.

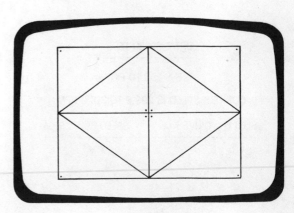

**FIG. 11–16**   Focus test screen.

*Williams: How to Repair & Maintain Your Apple Computer (Chilton)*

This test, accessed by selecting L, gives a more precise reading. It also allows you to make adjustments to the drive speed if these are necessary. The range should be between 299 and 301 rpm. The display shows you exact speed to within a tenth of an rpm (see Figure 11–17). This may vary slightly as the test runs, which is normal. If the variance is more than a few tenths, or if that variance takes place near the speed tolerance limit, it's time to adjust the drive speed. (See Chapter 4, "Drive Speed Adjustment.")

Be sure to use a diskette that contains no valuable data. It will be erased as the test runs. The test diskette you prepared in test D is fine for this purpose. If you have more than one drive, test each of them. Selection Q allows you to change the default drive.

## DISKETTE VERIFY TEST

Test M does two things at the same time. It checks the integrity of your DOS 3.3 formatted diskettes and the alignment of your heads.

The screen (Figure 11–18) shows an empty grid as you begin. Across the top, from left to right, are the track numbers. Going down the left-hand side are the sectors within each track. As the test runs, each sector on each track is checked. If that location is good, a dot will appear. If an error is found, a number will appear instead of the dot, indicating the number of times an error was found at that spot. If the diskette shows many errors scattered across the diskette, you have either a bad diskette or a malfunctioning drive. Reinitialize the diskette and try again. Test several other diskettes, especially ones you know to be good. If they fail continuously, chances are the drive is having trouble. (See Chapter 4.)

You can also test the alignment of two drives using this test. Initialize a

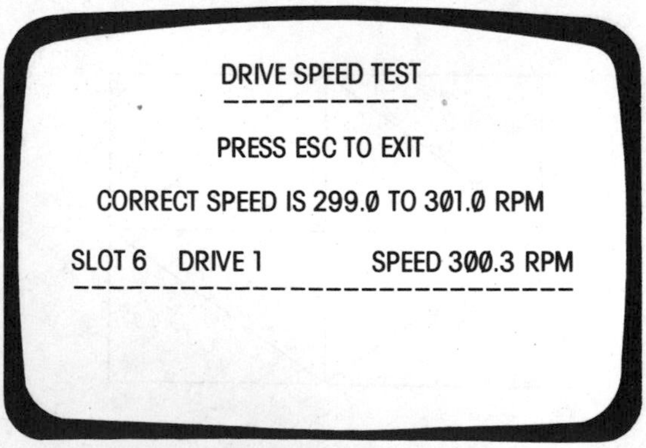

```
            DRIVE SPEED TEST
            -----------

            PRESS ESC TO EXIT

      CORRECT SPEED IS 299.0 TO 301.0 RPM

    SLOT 6    DRIVE 1          SPEED 300.3 RPM
    ------------------------------------
```

**FIG. 11–17** Drive speed test screen.

*Williams: How to Repair & Maintain Your Apple Computer (Chilton)*

```
                              DISKETTE VERIFY TEST
                              --------------------
        PRESS ESC TO RETURN TO MENU              PASS 0004
                                 TRACK
        SEC 000000000011111111112222222222233333
        TOR 012345678901234567890123456789012 34
        --------------------------------------------
          00  ........................................
          01  ........................................
          02  ........................................
          03  ........................................
          04  ........................................
          05  ........................................
          06  ........................................
          07  ........................................
          08  ........................................
          09  ........................................
          10  ........................................
          11  ........................................
          12  ........................................
          13  ........................................
          14  ........................................
          15  ........................................
```

**FIG. 11–18**  Diskette verify test screen.

diskette on one drive and test it. Then run the test on the same diskette in the second drive. The results should be identical. If not, one of the two may have a head alignment problem.

This testing routine is an excellent way to check the integrity of a diskette before you risk losing valuable data on it. It's a good idea to take a few extra minutes to test each new diskette you buy. Those with flaws on them (rare) can be weeded out before you find out the hard way that something is wrong with the diskette. But don't throw out the diskette until you've tried to initialize it at least once more.

## GAME CONTROLS TEST

Selection N from the main menu allows you to test the joysticks and paddles you have installed for games. The screen (Figure 11-19) is divided into two

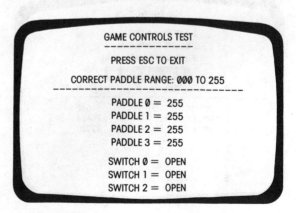

```
                    GAME CONTROLS TEST
                    ------------------
                     PRESS ESC TO EXIT

              CORRECT PADDLE RANGE: 000 TO 255
        -----------------------------------------
                      PADDLE 0 = 255
                      PADDLE 1 = 255
                      PADDLE 2 = 255
                      PADDLE 3 = 255

                      SWITCH 0 = OPEN
                      SWITCH 1 = OPEN
                      SWITCH 2 = OPEN
```

**FIG. 11–19**  Game controls test screen.

*Williams: How to Repair & Maintain Your Apple Computer (Chilton)*

parts. The top four listings, paddles 0 through 3, indicate movement of the paddle or joystick control. The reading should go between 0 and 255 as you move the control to the possible positions.

Beneath this are three switch listings, switches 0 to 2. This part of the display indicates whether the game control switches are working. Normal is OPEN. As you push the buttons, the screen should say CLOSED; as you release the buttons, the screen should say OPEN again.

For the IIe, the OPEN APPLE and CLOSED APPLE keys can be used as game controls. OPEN APPLE is represented on the screen by switch 0. CLOSED APPLE is represented by switch 1. As with testing joystick and paddle buttons, the reading on the screen should change from OPEN to CLOSED and back as you push and release the keys.


## ADD PERIPHERALS ROUTINE

Anytime you install, remove, or change a peripheral card, you have to run this routine. Otherwise you won't be able to test that card accurately in the future. Begin by entering O from the main menu.

On the screen (Figure 11–20), you are given three selections: (1) ADD NEW PERIPHERAL, (2) DELETE PERIPHERAL, and (3) RETURN TO MAIN MENU. Beneath this is a listing of what you have already told the program that you have installed, along with the signature code generated earlier by selection F (peripheral cards test). The numbers to the left of the entries do not necessarily indicate the slot number.

To add a new card, you must first run selection F with the new card in place. Then choose 1 and the cursor will move to the first available blank line.

**FIG. 11–20** Add peripherals screen.

*Williams: How to Repair & Maintain Your Apple Computer (Chilton)*

Type in a short description of the card you are installing, and press RETURN. The cursor will move to the signature column. Enter the signature code number that was generated when you ran F, and press RETURN. To add another new peripheral, choose 1 again and go through the same procedure.

To delete a card, select 2. The display will ask you, DELETE WHICH ENTRY NUMBER? If you wish to delete the listing for the card on line 3, merely type in 3, and press RETURN. To delete more than one card, select 2 again.

To exit this routine, select option 3. Don't forget to write down the signature number of the new cards.

## SUMMARY

A diagnostics program can be one of the most valuable pieces of software you own. It's not just for finding problems after they exist but also for keeping you informed of the general condition of your system. Running it should become a regular part of your maintenance schedule. The few extra minutes you'll spend each month are well worth it.

It's a good idea to run a diagnostics program while everything is working correctly. Don't just set it on the shelf until it is desperately needed. (This goes for any diagnostics program, not just the one used for this book.)

Keep a written record of the various test results. For example, what was the exact drive speed reading when you ran the test last? Has it changed, and if so, in which direction? A written record of the peripheral cards installed is very important, since you'll be referring to the signature code numbers to find out if there is a problem with a certain card.

# Write-Protect Sensor Program Appendix A

```
1      ***********************************
2      *                                 *
3      *          PROGRAM:               *
4      *      WRITE PROTECT SENSOR       *
5      *                                 *
6      * WRITTEN BY:                     *
7      *    JAMES N. WENNMACHER          *
8      *    7-31-84                      *
9      *                                 *
10     * THE PROGRAM READS THE STATUS    *
11     * OF THE WRITE PROTECT SWITCH     *
12     * ON THE SPECIFIED DRIVE AND      *
13     * PRINTS WHETHER OR NOT THE       *
14     * WRITE PROTECT SWITCH IS         *
15     * ENABLED OR DISABLED.            *
16     *                                 *
17     ***********************************
18     KEYBOARD EQU   $C000    ;KEYBOARD LOCATION
19     KBSTROBE EQU   $C010    ;KEYBOARD STROBE
20     HOME     EQU   $FC58    ;CLEARS TEXT SCREEN
21     COUT     EQU   $FDED    ;ROUTINE TO OUTPUT A CHAR
22     STARTING EQU   $2000    ;LOCATION TO LOAD PROGRAM
23     MSG      EQU   $FA      ;HOLDS ADDRESS OF MESSAGES
24     FLAG     EQU   $FA+2    ;FLAG FOR LAST SENSING
25     ***********************************
26     *                                 *
27     * MEMORY LOCATIONS FOR DRIVE      *
28     *                                 *
29     * NOTE : SLOT 6 IS ASSUMED        *
30     *                                 *
31     ***********************************
32     MOTOROFF EQU   $C0E8    ;TURN MOTOR OFF
33     MOTORON  EQU   $C0E9    ;TURN MOTOR ON
34     DRV1EN   EQU   $C0EA    ;ENGAGE DRIVE 1
35     Q6H      EQU   $C0ED    ;LOAD DATA LATCH
36     Q7L      EQU   $C0EE    ;PREPARE LATCH FOR INPUT
37                            ;Q6H + Q7L SENSES WRITE PROTECT
38     ***********************************
39     *                                 *
40     * BEGIN MAIN                      *
41     *                                 *
42     ***********************************
43              ORG   STARTING
```

```
2000: A9 20      44              LDA  #>STARTING  ;HIGH BYTE OF STARTING ADDRESS
2002: 85 FB      45              STA  MSG+1       ;SAVE IN PAGE 0
2004: A9 EA      46              LDA  #$EA        ;SELECT DRIVE 1
2006: 8D 29 20   47              STA  DRIVE+1     ;LATER IN PROGRAM
2009: A2 21      48              LDX  #MESG1-MESG0-1 ;GET LENGTH OF MESG0
200B: A9 66      49              LDA  #<MESG0     ;GET POSITION OF MESG0
200D: 20 B7 20   50              JSR  PRINT       ;PRINT MESG
2010: 20 C7 20   51              JSR  GETKEY      ;WAIT FOR KEY PRESS
2013: A2 12      52              LDX  #END-MESG3-1 ;PRINT MESG3
2015: A9 A4      53              LDA  #<MESG3
2017: 20 B7 20   54              JSR  PRINT
201A: 20 C7 20   55              JSR  GETKEY
201D: C9 B2      56              CMP  #"2"        ;WAS DRIVE 2 SELECTED?
201F: D0 03      57              BNE  CONTINUE    ;NO
2021: EE 29 20   58              INC  DRIVE+1
2024: A2 40      59  CONTINUE    LDX  #$40        ;BAD VALUE BECAUSE OVERFLOW IS
2026: 86 FC      60              STX  FLAG        ;SET, AND IT IS POSITIVE
2028: AD EA C0   61  DRIVE       LDA  DRV1EN      ;SELECT DRIVE 1
202B: AD E9 C0   62              LDA  MOTORON     ;TURN MOTOR ON TO READ SWITCH
202E: 2C 00 C0   63  SENSE       BIT  KEYBOARD    ;HAS A KEY BEEN PRESSED?
2031: 30 2A      64              BMI  DONE        ;YES
2033: AD ED C0   65              LDA  Q6H         ;SENSE WRITE PROTECT STATUS
2036: AD EE C0   66              LDA  Q7L
2039: 30 11      67              BMI  PROTECT     ;DISK PROTECTED
203B: 24 FC      68              BIT  FLAG        ;WAS WRITE ENABLED LAST TIME?
203D: 50 EF      69              BVC  SENSE       ;YES, DO NOTHING
203F: A2 00      70              LDX  #0          ;WRITE ENABLED
2041: 86 FC      71              STX  FLAG
2043: A2 0C      72              LDX  #MESG2-MESG1-1 ;PRINT MESG1
2045: A9 88      73              LDA  #<MESG1     ;LENGTH OF MESG1
2047: 20 B7 20   74              JSR  PRINT
204A: 30 E2      75              BMI  SENSE       ;CONTINUE SENSING WRITE PROTECT
204C: 24 FC      76  PROTECT     BIT  FLAG        ;WAS WRITE ENABLED LAST TIME?
204E: 30 DE      77              BMI  SENSE       ;NO
2050: A2 FF      78              LDX  #$FF
2052: 86 FC      79              STX  FLAG
2054: A2 0E      80              LDX  #MESG3-MESG2-1 ;PRINT MESG2
2056: A9 95      81              LDA  #<MESG2
2058: 20 B7 20   82              JSR  PRINT
205B: 30 D1      83              BMI  SENSE
205D: 8D E8 C0   84  DONE        STA  MOTOROFF    ;TURN OFF DRIVE MOTOR
2060: 8D 10 C0   85              STA  KBSTROBE    ;CLEAR KEYBOARD
2063: 4C D3 03   86              JMP  $3D3        ;RECONNECT DOS, ENTER BASIC
2066: CD C1 D2   87  MESG0       REV  "PRESS ANY KEY TO TERMINATE PROGRAM"
2069: C7 CF D2 D0 A0 C5 D4 C1
2071: CE C9 CD D2 C5 D4 A0 CF
2079: D4 A0 D9 C5 CB A0 D9 CE
2081: C1 A0 D3 D3 C5 D2 D0
2088: C4 C5 CC   88  MESG1       REV  "WRITE ENABLED"
208B: C2 C1 CE C5 A0 C5 D4 C9
2093: D2 D7
2095: C4 C5 D4   89  MESG2       REV  "WRITE PROTECTED"
2098: C3 C5 D4 CF D2 D0 A0 C5
```

```
20A0: D4 C9 D2 D7
20A4: B2 A0 D2  90    MESG3    REV   "SELECT DRIVE 1 OR 2"
20A7: CF A0 B1 A0 C5 D6 C9 D2
20AF: C4 A0 D4 C3 C5 CC C5 D3
                91    END
                92    ***********************************
                93    *                                 *
                94    *  SUBROUTINE PRINT               *
                95    *                                 *
                96    *  PRINTS THE MESSAGE INDEXED     *
                97    *  BY MSG.  LENGTH IN Y REG.      *
                98    *                                 *
                99    *  A, Y, AND STATUS REG ALTERED   *
               100    *                                 *
               101    ***********************************
20B7: 85 FA    102    PRINT    STA   MSG          ;SAVE POINTER TO PAGE 0
20B9: 20 58 FC 103             JSR   HOME
20BC: 8A       104             TXA                ;PUT MESG LENGTH IN Y
20BD: A8       105             TAY
20BE: B1 FA    106    PRINTLP  LDA   (MSG),Y      ;GET CHAR
20C0: 20 ED FD 107             JSR   COUT         ;PRINT
20C3: 88       108             DEY
20C4: 10 F8    109             BPL   PRINTLP
20C6: 60       110             RTS
               111    ***********************************
               112    *                                 *
               113    *  SUBROUTINE GETKEY              *
               114    *                                 *
               115    *  WAITS FOR A KEY TO BE PRESSED*
               116    *                                 *
               117    *  A AND STATUS REG ALTERED       *
               118    *                                 *
               119    ***********************************
20C7: AD 00 C0 120    GETKEY   LDA   KEYBOARD     ;LOOK AT KEYBOARD
20CA: 10 FB    121             BPL   GETKEY       ;NO KEY PRESSED YET
20CC: 8D 10 C0 122             STA   KBSTROBE     ;CLEAR KEYBOARD
20CF: 60       123             RTS
```

Symbol table - alphabetical order:

```
CONTINUE=$2024    COUT    =$FDED    DONE    =$205D    DRIVE    =$2028
DRV1EN  =$C0EA    END     =$20B7    FLAG    =$FC      GETKEY   =$20C7
HOME    =$FC58    KBSTROBE=$C010    KEYBOARD=$C000    MESG0    =$2066
MESG1   =$2088    MESG2   =$2095    MESG3   =$20A4    MOTOROFF =$C0E8
MOTORON =$C0E9    MSG     =$FA      PRINT   =$20B7    PRINTLP  =$20BE
PROTECT =$204C    Q6H     =$C0ED    Q7L     =$C0EE    SENSE    =$202E
STARTING=$2000
```

Symbol table - numerical order:

```
MSG     =$FA      FLAG     =$FC      STARTING=$2000    CONTINUE=$2024
DRIVE   =$2028    SENSE    =$202E    PROTECT =$204C    DONE    =$205D
MESG0   =$2066    MESG1    =$2088    MESG2   =$2095    MESG3   =$20A4
END     =$20B7    PRINT    =$20B7    PRINTLP =$20BE    GETKEY  =$20C7
KEYBOARD=$C000    KBSTROBE =$C010    MOTOROFF=$C0E8    MOTORON =$C0E9
DRV1EN  =$C0EA    Q6H      =$C0ED    Q7L     =$C0EE    HOME    =$FC58
COUT    =$FDED
```

==

# IIe Self-Test
# Appendix B

The following information about the IIe self-test is courtesy of Apple Computer, Inc.

## RUNNING THE SELF-TEST

1. Connect the power supply and the monitor to the logic board.
2. Plug in the power supply and turn it on.
   The power LED on the logic board (near the power supply connector) should come on, the monitor should alternate between white and black about every five seconds (black most of the time), and the self-test LED near the video connector should be on.
   Note: The self-test LED is in parallel with the speaker connector. If you were to connect the speaker, it would buzz and the LED would be out.
3. Turn the power off.
4. Connect the keyboard and the speaker to the logic board.
5. Turn the power on.
   The power LED on the logic board should come on, as should the power lamp on the keyboard. You should hear a single beep, and the monitor should display the APPLE ][ logo at the top, the Applesoft prompt ] near

*Williams: How to Repair & Maintain Your Apple Computer (Chilton)*

the top at the left edge, and a blinking checkerboard cursor just right of the prompt.

6. Hold down the CONTROL key, then press and release the RESET key, and then release the CONTROL key.

    You should hear a single beep, the original prompt should scroll up to the top of the screen and the logo should scroll off the top, and a second prompt should appear, with the blinking cursor, at the bottom.

    This tests the manual reset function.

7. Press and hold the RETURN key.

    A line of prompts should start "growing" up the left edge.

    This tests the autorepeat function.

8. Release the RETURN key.

9. Hold down the CONTROL and CLOSED APPLE keys, press and release the RESET key, and then release the CONTROL and CLOSED APPLE keys.

    The screen should alternate between black and white twice and then display the message KERNEL OK. This should take a total of about 15 seconds.

*Williams: How to Repair & Maintain Your Apple Computer (Chilton)*

+------------------------------------------------------------------+
|                            WARNING                                |
|                                                                   |
|  If anyone but an authorized Apple service representative tries    |
|  to repair an Apple product, both the Limited Warranty and, if    |
|  purchased, the AppleCare service contract become void, and the   |
|  user must pay for all labor and parts needed to repair that       |
|  product.                                                         |
+------------------------------------------------------------------+

## DIAGNOSTICS ERRORS

The following is a list of self-test errors.

Look at the sample error message IOU FLAG E5:1. It is broken down into the test being run when the error was detected (IOU [input/output unit] flag test), the location of the suspect IC (E5), and the error type (1). In this example, an IOU error 1 means that an incorrect state of the Mixed Mode switch was detected.

If more than one error occurred, they would be listed after the colon. For example, IOU FLAG E5:1 3 means that errors 1 and 3 were detected.

### MMU ERRORS

The first tests done by the diagnostics are the MMU (main memory unit) ECS (environmental control switch) flag tests. Whenever an error occurs during testing of the MMU, the error prefix MMU FLAG E4: followed by one or more hexadecimal characters is output. An example of an MMU failure message is:

MMU FLAG E4:2 5 C

The error text notes that only ECS flags are tested. From this text you can see that the MMU has failed, the MMU is at location E4, and errors 2, 5, and C were detected.

A description of the errors follows (assume positive logic: asserted = 1, negated = 0):
Error 0 RDLCBANKO (read language card bank zero status).
    If asserted, this signal banks in the first $D000 bank on the langauge
        card.
    Read at $C011.
    On reset this signal should be asserted; it was found to be negated.
Error 1 RDLCRDRAM (read language card read RAM status).
    This flag, if asserted, means that you are looking at the language card
        RAM and the ROM is banked out.

Williams: *How to Repair & Maintain Your Apple Computer* (Chilton)

Read at $C012.

On reset this signal should be negated; it was found to be asserted.

Error 2 RDRAMRD (read RAM read status).

This flag, if asserted, means that the machine is reading the other 64K bank on the 80-column card.

Read at $C013.

On reset this signal should be negated; it was found to be asserted.

Error 3 RDRAMWRT (read RAM write status).

This flag, if asserted, means that the machine is doing RAM writes to the other 64K bank on the 80-column card.

Read at $C014.

On reset this signal should be negated; it was found to be asserted.

Error 4 RDCXROM (read CX ROM status).

If RDCXROM is asserted, the slots are not accessible and the ROM "behind" the slots is banked in.

Read at $C015.

On reset this signal should be asserted; it was found to be negated.

Error 5 RDZP (read zero page status).

RDZP, when asserted, will cause the machine to perform its zero page transactions on the zero page in the 64K RAM bank on the 80-column card.

Read at $C016.

On reset this signal should be negated; it was found to be asserted.

Error 6 RDC3ROM (read status of ROM behind slot 3).

RDC3ROM, when asserted, will cause slot 3 to be banked out and the ROM from $C300 to $C3FF to be banked in.

Read at $C017.

On reset this signal should be asserted; it was found to be negated.

Error 7 RD80STORE (read 80-column store status).

When RD80STORE is asserted, 1K of memory on the 80-column card is banked into the normal text buffer at $0400–$07FF.

Read at $C018.

On reset this signal should be negated; it was found to be asserted.

The following errors are encountered if an ECS cannot be toggled to its non-reset state.

Error 8 RDLCBANK0

When address $C08B was referenced, RDLCBANK0 did not change state.

Error 9 RDLCRDRAM

When address $C080 was referenced, RDLCRDRAM did not change state.

*Williams: How to Repair & Maintain Your Apple Computer (Chilton)*

Error A RDRAMRD

When address $C003 was written to, RDRAMRD did not change state.

Error B RDRAMWRT

When address $C005 was written to, RDRAMWRT did not change state.

Error C RDZP

When address $C009 was written to, RDZP did not change state.

Error D RDC3ROM

When address $C00B was written to, RDC3ROM did not change state.

Error E RD80STORE

When address $C001 was written to, RD80STORE did not change state.

## IOU ERRORS

The next tests done by the diagnostics are the IOU ECS tests. The failure messages for the IOU are in the same format as those for the MMU. An example of an IOU failure message is:

IOU FLAG E5:0 4 B

Error 0 RDTEXT (read test mode status).

This flag, when asserted, indicates that the machine is in text mode.

Read at $C01A.

On reset this flag should be asserted; it was found to be negated.

Error 1 RDMIXMODE (read graphics Mixed Mode status).

When asserted, RDMIXMODE indicates that MIX is in effect.

Read at $C01B.

On reset this flag should be negated; it was found to be asserted.

Error 2 RDPAGE2 (read display page status).

When RDPAGE2 is asserted, it indicates that the second page of the display is displayed.

Read at $C01C.

On reset this flag should be negated; it was found to be asserted.

Error 3 RDHIRES (read high-resolution graphics status).

RDHIRES is asserted when HIRES graphics is displayed.

Read at $C01D.

On reset this flag should be negated; it was found to be asserted.

Error 4 RDALTCHAR (read alternate character set status).

When RDALTCHAR is asserted, the standard character set is replaced by a character set that adds full set inverse capability at the expense of flashing characters.

Read at $C01E.

On reset this flag should be negated; it was found to be asserted.

Error 5 RD80VID (read 80-column video status).
> When asserted, RD80VID indicates 80-column mode is in effect.
> Read at $C01F.
> On reset this flag should be negated; it was found to be asserted.

The following errors are encountered if an ECS cannot be toggled to its non-reset state.

Error 6 RD80VID
> When address $C00D was written to, RD80VID did not change state.

Error 7 RDALTCHAR
> When address $C00F was written to, RDALTCHAR did not change state.

Error 8 RDTEXT
> When address $C050 (GR) was referenced, RDTEXT did not change state.

Error 9 RDPAGE2
> When address $C055 was referenced, RDPAGE2 did not change state.

Error A RDMIXMODE
> When address $C053 was referenced, RDMIXMODE did not change state.

Error B RDHIRES
> When address $C057 was referenced, RDHIRES did not change state.

## ROM ERRORS

The ROM test in the diagnostics consists of a checksum test on both the CD and EF ROM chips. If a ROM chip fails, you will see one of the following messages:

ROM:E8 or ROM:E10

The messages indicate that a ROM chip failed the checksum test and should be replaced.

## RAM ERRORS

The RAM test is an N-pattern test that will take about seven seconds to complete. The RAM test will check all 64K of memory in the Apple IIe (language card tests are included). The RAM test is a four-pass, march-type test that checks the following RAM functions:

1. Ability to store a one and a zero at every location
2. Uniqueness of all addresses

*Williams: How to Repair & Maintain Your Apple Computer (Chilton)*

3. Refresh operation
4. Banking functions in the language card

If a failure is detected in the RAM, the prefix RAM: followed by the coordinates of the failing RAM chip(s) will be output. An example of a RAM failure might be:

RAM:F13 F7 F6

Remember that the RAM test depends on a small portion of RAM working. Sometimes multiple RAM failures are caused by only one bad chip.

# Glossary

**AC:** Alternating current measured in cycles per second (cps) or hertz. The standard value coming through the wall outlet is 120 volts at 60 hertz. This voltage passes through a fuse or circuit breaker that can handle about 15 amps (check for yourself). The Apple can tolerate an AC value of between 107 volts and 132 volts. The power supply changes this to the proper DC levels required by the computer.

**Access:** A fancy term for "to get at."

**Acoustic:** Having to do with sound waves. For example, an acoustic modem sends and receives data as a series of audible beeps. (A direct-connected modem is better because it is not prone to interference or false signals from room noise.)

**Address:** Location of a particular piece of data or other information in the computer. (See Chapter 5.) Can also refer to the location of set of instructions.

**ASCII:** American Standard Code for Information Interchange. This code assigns binary (on/off) values to the 7-bit capability of the computer. The 8th bit signals the end of the character or functions as a parity bit to check for errors. ASCII is the standard code used to send data and other binary information (e.g., through a telephone modem).

**Asynchronous:** Often abbreviated *asynch*. Refers to communications mode in which each character is balanced individually (e.g., with a stop bit). Communications occurs in only one direction at a time; one command must be completed before the next is performed.

**Audio:**  A signal that can be heard (through the speaker of the Apple, for example).

**Backup:**  A copy of a program or data diskette. Make them often to protect yourself.

**Bank:**  The collection of memory modules that make up a block of 16K in the RAM (64K in the IIe)—usually eight ICs.

**BASIC:**  One of the most common first-learned computer languages. The Apple has four versions: *Applesoft* and *Integer*, both available as either cassette or diskette versions. Cassette BASIC resides in the ROM and is loaded automatically if no drive controller card is present. Disk BASIC is on the DOS diskette.

**Baud:**  Used to describe the speed of transmission. The signal is split into a certain number of parts per second. Thus 300 baud will send 300 units per second. Generally each unit is a bit; 300 baud basically means that 300 bits per second are being sent.

**Bit:**  A single pulse (on/off) of information used in binary code. The word *bit* is actually the abbreviation for *binary digit*.

**Boot:**  To load a program into the computer. The term comes from *bootstrap*, which in turn comes from *lifting oneself by one's own bootstraps*. It means that the computer is loading itself and setting itself to operate, without operator intervention.

**Buffer:**  A segment of memory used to store data temporarily while the data is being transferred from one device to another. A common example is a printer buffer. This device stores the incoming data at full computer speed (9,600 baud) and sends it to the printer at a speed at which the printer can use it (such as 40 characters per second, or about 300 baud). Another example is the buffer used by DOS 3.3 in transferring material to and from the disk drive.

**Bug:**  An error in a program.

**Byte:**  A collection of bits that makes up a character or other designation. Generally a byte is 8 data bits, the binary representation of a character.

**Carrier:**  The reference signal used for the transmission or reception of data. The most common use with computers involves modem communications over phone lines. The modem monitors this signal to tell if the data is coming through. Generally, if the carrier isn't getting through, neither is the data.

**Catalog:**  The allocation track of a diskette. Stores the titles given to the files saved on the diskette and tells the computer and drives how to get to those

*Williams: How to Repair & Maintain Your Apple Computer (Chilton)*

files. The directory serves as a "Table of Contents" for the files saved on the diskette. The catalog sorts file identification data by name, size, type (e.g., Applesoft, Integer, text, or binary file), the date the file was created (with ProDOS), and the data that the computer needs to find that file on the diskette. With ProDOS, the directory file indicates if the file is locked or not.

**Chip:**   Another name for an IC, or integrated circuit.

**Circuit:**   A complete electronic path.

**Circuit board:**   The collection of circuits gathered together on a sheet of phrenolic plastic, usually with all contacts made through a strip of pins. The circuit board is generally made by chemically etching metal-coated phrenolic plastic.

**Common:**   The ground or return path used in this book to make measurements with the multimeter. The black probe.

**CPU:**   Central processing unit.

**CRT:**   Cathode ray tube; basically a fancy name for a television or monitor screen tube.

**Crystal:**   A small device located on various boards (on the bottom left corner of the mother board) that vibrates at a particular frequency. One use is as a reference frequency for timing circuits.

**Data:**   Information.

**DC:**   Direct current, such as that provided by the power supply. (Also found in batteries.)

**Debug:**   To rid a program of errors, or bugs.

**Default:**   An assumption the computer makes when no other parameters are specified. For example, if you type CATALOG without specifying which drive to search, the computer automatically goes to the default drive (normally the last one selected) and assumes that this is what you want. If you have selected drive 2, this is the default drive until you select drive 1 again. The term is used in software to describe any action the computer or program takes on its own with embedded values.

**Density:**   The amount of information that can be stored per unit area on a diskette. Diskettes used for the Apple are single density (and single sided).

**Directory:**   (See **Catalog.**)

**Diskette:**   The flat magnetically coated media used in computers for the storage of data.

**DOS:**   Disk Operating System. Most common for the Apple are DOS 3.3, and ProDOS, and CP/M.

**Drive:**   The device used to read and write on diskettes. With the Apple, the primary drive is 1 and the secondary drive is 2. If the drive is "fixed," it is commonly called a hard drive or "Winchester" drive. The drive can also be electronic, using available RAM instead of the magnetic media.

**DSDD:**   Double sided, double density. Describes the diskettes used in a double-sided drive. These are not used by Apple.(*See* **SSSD.**)

**Edit:**   To change or modify data.

**Emulate:**   A fancy word for "pretend to be." Often used to describe a device that is designed to make the computer *seem* to be another computer or terminal.

**Execute:**   To start a program or instruction set.

**FAT:**   Files Allocation Table. An area on the diskette used to allocate space for files. The information included in the table indicates which sectors on the diskette are free and which are used.

**FCC:**   Federal Communications Commission. Regulates the kind and amount of radio frequencies that can be emitted by computers and computer devices.

**Ferric oxide:**   The iron substance most often used as the magnetic medium on diskettes. ($Fe_2O_3$) Essentially it is nothing more than rusted iron.

**File:**   Any collection of information saved on a diskette. The file can consist of data, programs, or both.

**Firmware:**   The ROM of the computer.

**Flippy:**   A diskette with notches and index holes cut into both sides, allowing both sides of the diskette to be used by a single-sided drive (by flipping the diskette over).

**Font:**   A style of lettering. Many matrix printers can use a variety of print styles, changeable through software.

**Format:**   A command within DOS (INIT) that assigns various tracks and sectors to new diskettes. Also, a particular manner in which something is laid out, such as in a program. (*See also* **INIT.**)

**Ground:**   The common or return side of a circuit. (*See also* **Common.**)

**Hardware:**   The computer and computer devices.

**Head:**   The read/write head of the disk drive.

**HELLO:**   The program that is run when a disk is first booted up and that automatically loads the working program. The name of this file can be changed by the Master Create program on the DOS diskette or by the INIT command.

**Hertz (Hz):**   A measure of frequency. One cycle per second (cps). Frequency is also measured in units such as kilohertz (KHz—thousands of cycles per second) and megahertz (MHz—millions of cycles per second).

**Hub ring:**   A plastic reinforcing ring applied to the spindle access hole of a diskette. This ring adds strength and improves centering.

**IC:** Integrated circuit. This is a package of electronics, often encased in black plastic, with pins coming from the bottom. Pin 1 is the first pin on the right on the side with the notch or other marking.

**Index hole:** Small hole on the diskette near the hub access hole; used by some computers to find the beginning of a sector. Not used by the Apple.

**INIT:** The command in DOS that tells DOS to format (prepare) a diskette so that data can be recorded on it. The name after the INIT command is the name of the file that DOS will try to run when the disk is loaded. .

**Interface:** A fancy term to say *connect*. Used to describe any connection from hardware to hardware, hardware to software, and even hardware or software to user.

**K:** With computers, usually used to describe an amount of memory. Generally K denotes 1,000 (as in kilohertz). Because of the electronics involved, 1K of memory is actually 1,024 bytes; 64K is actually 65,536 bytes.

**Keyboard:** Primary means of manual input to a computer.

**LED:** Light-emitting diode, such as those used in the drives to indicate that the spindle is turning.

**Light pen:** An instrument designed to read areas on the screen by pointing at them. Enables input of data to the computer in a manner similar to that of a mouse (*see* **Mouse**); used in addition to or instead of a keyboard.

**Matrix:** A pattern of dots, in computer printers used to make up letters, numbers, and other symbols.

**Minifloppy:** Still another name for a diskette. Describes a $5\frac{1}{4}$-inch floppy.

**Modem:** A device for transmitting data over telephone lines. The name means *modulate-demodulate*.

**Monitor:** A televisionlike device to display characters and other symbols. Also called a display, CRT, or VDU.

**Mouse:** A handheld device rolled across a surface in order to input data to the computer. Often used to get quickly from one spot on the screen to another. The name comes from the small size of the device, the tail-like cable, and the two buttons that (to some people) resemble eyes.

**Multimeter:** A testing device to measure volts and ohms across a variety of ranges. Often called a VOM.

**Ohm:** Unit of measurement of resistance.

**Operating system:** DOS.

**Parallel:** Refers to a means of data transfer in which information is sent a byte at a time. (*See also* **Serial.**)

**Parity:** A means of error checking. Mainly used in communications on the Apple. Parity checking can be even or odd. Even parity checking means

*Williams: How to Repair & Maintain Your Apple Computer (Chilton)*

that the number of 1 bits (on) in a byte must be even. Odd parity means that the number of 1 bits in a byte must be odd.

**Platen:**   The rubber roller of the printer.

**Polyethylene terephthalate:**   The generic name of the material used to make diskettes. Common trademark name is Mylar.

**Port:**   A place where cables are connected to the computer or other device. Sometimes called an interface.

**Power-on reset:**   This is the 74LS74 chip located at A-11 on the mother board of the II and II+. It is part of ROM in the IIe.

**ProDOS:**   The newest DOS available from Apple at this time. Unlike previous versions, ProDOS is designed to handle systems that use hard drives.

**Program:**   A set of instructions the computer can understand and act upon to perform a task.

**Prompt:**   A symbol on the screen indicating a state of readiness in the computer (e.g., ], >, !, or *). It's waiting for you to do something.

**Sector:**   An area on the track of the diskette assigned to hold a certain amount of information. In the Apple, each sector is assigned to hold 256 bytes of information. DOS 3.2 assigns 13 sectors per track; DOS 3.3 and ProDOS assign 16 sectors per track. The logical unit with ProDOS, however, is a block, which is composed of 2 sectors.

**Serial:**   A means of data transfer in which information is handled a bit (or pulse) at a time, with each bit following the others.

**Soft sector:**   A method of setting up a diskette (through the INIT command) so that data is written first to a sector whose position is determined by a code stored on disk.

**Software:**   Computer programs, usually on diskette or cassette.

**Source:**   Where a signal originates.

**Spindle:**   The device in the disk drives that is inserted into the center hole and causes the diskette to spin.

**SSSD:**   Single sided, single density. Describes diskettes used in the Apple drives.

**Stepper motor:**   Used to move the read/write heads across the surface of the diskette.

**System board:**   The main circuit board of the Apple. More correctly called the mother board.

**Target:**   Where a signal is to terminate. For example, if you are copying a file, the target is the diskette on which the file is to be copied.

**Terminal:**   In a computer system, a device through which data can be entered or retrieved. Can also be the end point of an electrical connection. Sometimes used to describe a monitor (i.e., video terminal).

*Williams: How to Repair & Maintain Your Apple Computer (Chilton)*

**TPI:**   Tracks per inch. Standard with the Apple is 48 TPI, with 35 tracks used.

**Track:**   One of the concentric rings on a diskette. The Apple uses 35 tracks, each holding either 13 or 16 sectors depending on the DOS being used (see **Sector**), with each sector holding 256 bytes of information.

**TVI:**   Television interference. Computers and some computer devices emit radio frequencies that can interfere with normal television operation.

**VOM:**   Volt-ohm-milliammeter. Commonly called a multimeter.

**Write-protect:**   The notch cut into the diskette that allows a switch in the drive to activate the recording head. With this notch covered, the recording head is disabled, making recording on the diskette impossible.

# Index